Visiting Wallace

EDITED BY

DENNIS BARONE AND

JAMES FINNEGAN

visiting wallace

Poems Inspired by the Life and Work of Wallace Stevens

University of Iowa Press

Iowa City

University of Iowa Press, Iowa City 52242

www.uiowapress.org
Printed in the United States of America

Design by April Leidig-Higgins

The University of Iowa Press is a member of Green
Press Initiative and is committed to preserving natural
resources.

Printed on acid-free paper

Library of Congress Cataloging-in-Publication Data
Visiting Wallace: poems inspired by the life and work
of Wallace Stevens / edited by Dennis Barone and
James Finnegan.
       p.   cm.
Includes index.
ISBN-13: 978-1-58729-811-0 (pbk.)
ISBN-10: 1-58729-811-2 (pbk.)
1. Stevens, Wallace, 1879–1955 — Poetry.   2. Stevens,
Wallace, 1879–1955 — Parodies, imitations, etc.
3. Poets — Poetry.   I. Barone, Dennis.   II. Finnegan,
James, 1955–
PS3537.T4753Z826   2009   2009005394
811'.52 — dc22

Contents

Descriptions without Places

Many poets who are devoted readers of Wallace Stevens are charmed and even seduced by the quiet house on a weekday evening, the reader in his chair, the sullen man sitting at the end of his bed, the ordinariness that constituted Stevens's quiet suburban life — often, in the poems, the implied scene of composition that serves as the starting point for wild flights of imagination. Dennis Barone, one of our editors, captures this sense in the very words and phrases he chooses for "An Ordinary Evening": *empty, quiet, large, slightly, nothing remains, dried out, sits, awaits, dreams, stretches forth, distant.* Most of the poems assembled here comprehend this — what is it, really? — disaffected intensity.

The disaffection is a marvel, since it prevents a definitive legacy. The man in the room in the house is sufficiently vague in his love of mundane things to enable poetic identities across the landscape, inside and out. Sitting quietly in his chair, he and we are everywhere and nowhere. His style functions likewise.

Indeed, seventy-six poems give us seventy-six distinct Stevenses to follow and succeed. Is there another modern poet who means this many distinct things to contemporary verse? Meet all these aesthetic selves in the words of those whom he — *they* — influenced. Here is the man hard to love, beloved nonetheless (in Robert Bly's tribute); the poet so rhetorically overwhelming that one cannot help but fall into his demotic yet abstract vocabulary ("mak[ing] all acquiesce to one's preeminent premise," says Creeley); the modernist who's gotten so completely under later poets' skins that satire (as in Mark DeFoe's "Thirteen Ways of Eradicating Blackbirds") seems the only poetic recourse; the lonely lover joining the most intense rendezvous of paramours who are exactly as strange to themselves as to society (in John Ashbery's truly great poem, "Some

Trees"); the personage to be awed (as in Richard Eberhart's memory of drinking pitchers of martinis with the great poet at the Canoe Club); the businessman-poet who made money but also contemplated his rich idiomatic life (in Dana Gioia's formal riff); the Edward Hopperesque purveyor of hard flat surfaces (per Tony Quagliano); the theorist of nothingness who makes us think plentifully (per Jerome Sala); the man with the tropical imagination (Lisa M. Steinman); the language philosopher (in Michael Palmer's brilliant lyric on "linear inquiry"); the tragic composer (David St. John); the man made of words (R. S. Thomas); the landscape colorist (Charles Tomlinson), the urbanist (Lewis Turco); the citizen who lives nowhere (William Carlos Williams); and, back in the house, the room-to-room wanderer (Susan Howe).

The implicit generosity of what Barone and Finnegan have done in this volume will widen and extend our approaches to a poet whose effect on us is never as clear as that of Whitman, Pound, Dickinson, or Ginsberg. In *Visiting Emily*, disconcerting and exciting as it is, we nonetheless know what possibility we're dwelling in, and we land on the room's floor with both feet. In *Visiting Wallace*, we stay (in Howe's words) "on tiptoe" and "do not infringe."

Introduction

Visiting Wallace: there is something incongruous about such a title. Elsie Stevens may have frequently filled the house with fresh roses from the garden, but seldom did the Stevens family welcome guests into their home. The current residents of the large brick and clapboard house on Westerly Terrace in Hartford are known for hosting an annual backyard pig roast. Lest we forget, Wallace Stevens was a vice president at the Hartford Livestock Insurance Company as well as the Hartford Accident and Indemnity Company.

Stevens cherished his solitude. As he wrote to his friend Barbara Church, "Hartford is quiet. There is a loneliness and a thoughtfulness about everything which I like, as if all interruptions had come to an end." Stevens told another friend, Hi Simons, "I am not a good talker and don't particularly enjoy exchanging ideas with people in talk. At home [as a child in Reading, Pennsylvania], our house was rather a curious place, with all of us in different parts of it, reading."

And so we hope the seventy-six poems gathered here are neither intrusion nor interruption but just the ticket for retreating to a corner of your own house and entering into a kind of conversation among poets. You can visit then through the printed page and not by physical presence, though some of the poems herein may make palpable a sense of that place and that person who lived there. Other poems in this collection may serve as a poetic criticism or interpretation of a particular work of Stevens, and some may evoke the Stevensian colors of red and green and blue. Others may simply tell a good joke. And while many poems refer to either Stevens's home life or his writing, only a few refer to his work as a lawyer for an insurance company. "The essential poem," Stevens wrote in "A Primitive Like an Orb," "begets the others," and all the works in this gathering show just how essential Stevens's poetry is for us now.

Stevens once wrote from Greensboro, North Carolina, to his wife in Hartford: "This hotel is named after O. Henry, the writer of short stories, who came from Greensboro. Such is fame. Fancy having your name on the soup ladle, on all the linen, shrimps O. Henry, salad O. Henry, parfait O. Henry. There's an O. Henry cigar, an O. Henry drug store, and so on." Stevens called this chain of naming "absurd hero-worship."

Meanwhile, the O. Henry ending has become a cliché — even in Greensboro, while Stevens's reputation has soared. As the poet R. S. Thomas concludes his contribution to this book of seventy-six poems (one for each year of Stevens's life, plus one more for good measure):

> I stand with my back to grammar
> at an altar you never aspired
> to, celebrating the sacrament
> of the imagination whose high-priest
> notwithstanding you are.

No other American poet, we would argue, has been more influential upon American poets during the past thirty years than Stevens. As Susan Howe, one of the contributors to the present anthology, told us, "Wallace Stevens is my necessary angel. If he hadn't existed, I would have had to invent him." Similarly, Robert Kelly wrote to us that Stevens "is the necessary (not angel but) thoughtful argument we must always wage against the lyric isolate. So much of my work honors (if I may flatter myself) him and his." And in the recent *Poet's Bookshelf* anthologies, more poets cited work by Wallace Stevens for its significance in shaping their poetic art than work by any other writer.

The poems in this anthology come from all stages of poets' writing careers. Some have been written especially for this volume and some are many decades old. Maureen Owen based her poem on "Anecdote of the Jar," a poem that led her to Stevens when she was a teenager. "It was one of the very first poems I memorized," she told us. "I find myself continually returning to it. It rather haunts me." "Thirteen Ways of Looking at a Blackbird" seems to be a favorite for poets to satirize, and "Sunday Morning" evokes a more solemn response. Poets herein have either entered into dialogue with Stevens in general or with one particular poem. As Forrest Gander wrote to us, "At the end of 'Sunday Morning' . . . a voice again cries and Stevens follows it with his incredible, 'We live in an old chaos of the sun.' My poem ends with the two lines that ask about whose voice is the voice that is heard. And the sun is parsed as 'glorious, unstrung light.' My poem continues, and continues to stay in dialogue with Stevens." Other poems herein show their Stevensian influence in an indirect manner.

We have included in this collection only poems originally written in English and only one poem per poet. The alphabetical organization makes for some surprising juxtapositions, smooth transitions, or emphatic repetitions. For us, one of the joys gained in assembling *Visiting Wallace* has been the range of poets — with so many different aesthetic perspectives — who have stopped by to visit, to offer tribute. We hope that you will enjoy reading poems rich in humor as well as ones sonorous with melody; poems driven by their subject matter as well as ones that probe the manner of their speaking. Readers, there is pleasure and insight aplenty herein. Come, celebrate with us the genius of Wallace Stevens's life and work through the engagement of seventy-six poets.

We heartily thank Saint Joseph College for a generous contribution toward the many permission fees for this volume. We would also like to acknowledge the assistance of Kathleen Kelley of the Saint Joseph College Library and our fellow board members of the Hartford Friends and Enemies of Wallace Stevens: Karim Ahmed, Lonnie Black, John Orofino, Christine Palm, Dan Schnaidt, Phil Tegeler, and the late Hugh Ogden. Lastly, we thank John Serio of the *Wallace Stevens Journal* for printing so many poems inspired by the life and work of Wallace Stevens.

Visiting Wallace

Memo from the Desk of Wallace Stevens:

Send me a postcard from
Chile or Tunis to
Tape on my dresser or
Sail through my office.

Let it be frightfully
Luscious or smashing for
Nightmares or psalm-sings and
Scribbles of pencils.

Find me flamingos and
Cats in the jungles with
Faces like moochers who
Thrust out their fingers.

Mail it from beaches where
Waves look like forestry
Ghosts in their gullies that
Waltz in the shadows.

Florida charms me — its
Keys with their looping toward
Cuba, their coral, their
Fishermen bronzing.

Yet, for my needs, if you're
Touring Morocco and
Chance by a view of a
Harbor or ruin,

Post it to Hartford where
I shall be waiting to
Sweeten the world with my
Blackberry mind.

⎯

Dear Wallace

I begin where you leave off, that palm
beyond which the real has not yet formed
that place/time always raw, just grasping
what is not quite there, the demon
trembling in the hedge, the far thought
running just out of range, pink foot visible
at the entrance to the maze.
Here is where you lived even in a suit,
boxed at the office, the linen flower
of your public self, and here, beyond which
always, like a mouse trapped in the pantry,
that which would not become *respectable*
hid among those bourgeois props and bric-a-brac,
and yes, at the club, seated with cognac
among men who would not know a poem
from the filigree engraving on their Purdeys,
you still composed, between skeet range
and greenhouse, the high sheened mind's
corona and flame, the jeweled and captured spirit.
You were like the naked man in the dream
walking happily among flowers until you saw
the priest, the matron or the law, frowning,
and covered yourself in shame. How much harder
for us who refuse to hide the raw elixir.
In our world without shame (and shameless)
we cannot draw steam from
the pot you kept covered. Everything
dissipates. The walls between
the hidden and the naked self dissolve.

Some Trees

These are amazing: each
Joining a neighbor, as though speech
Were a still performance.
Arranging by chance

To meet as far this morning
From the world as agreeing
With it, you and I
Are suddenly what the trees try

To tell us we are:
That their merely being there
Means something; that soon
We may touch, love, explain.

And glad not to have invented
Such comeliness, we are surrounded:
A silence already filled with noises,
A canvas on which emerges

A chorus of smiles, a winter morning.
Placed in a puzzling light, and moving,
Our days put on such reticence
These accents seem their own defense.

Quarry

No more than the song of it. As if
the singing alone
had led us back to this place.

We have been here, and we have never been here.
We have been on the way to where we began,
and we have been lost.

There are no boundaries
in the light. And the earth
leaves no word for us
to sing. For the crumbling of the earth
underfoot

is a music in itself, and to walk among these stones
is to hear nothing
but ourselves.

I sing, therefore, of nothing,

as if it were the place
I do not return to —

and if I should return, then count out my life
in these stones: forget
I was ever here. The world
that walks inside me

is a world beyond reach.

Poussiniana

An early morning's complete Poussiniana.
— Wallace Stevens

Twenty-four panes to the window,
A hand of water rolling on its axis,
And waterfowl on Burnham Pond, preening.
He lifts the saw to the wounded limb.
Moss on the oak, leaves on the lawn.
The angelsbreath bowing the air,
The cat watching a bee
Bang against the glass.
There's this, there's that.

There is so much here to remember
You forget the waxing Sunday afternoon
Or the geraniums growing beside you.
You forget that there are deep sumps in the far hills,
You forget the overlaid tornado tracks,
You forget Carrie Foster, who owns the woods,
Who dresses like men and who lives alone.
You forget about Tempe Wicke, who hid her horse
In her bedroom from the rebels —
All this, all that.

The present is just this once,
The limb is meeting the ground,
You can hear the earthworm
Heaving
In the garden.

An Ordinary Evening

His house is empty when
He arrives — empty and
Quiet and large. Perhaps,

It is too large for one man
And two women. From
The window of his study

He can look toward the town
He travels to each morning
And returns from each night.

It is winter and the slope of
His yard, so green six months
Ago, is now awash in white,

Patterned slightly by the paws
Of the neighbor's cat. Of the
Garden nothing remains but

The dried out sticks of roses
Trimmed low to the ground
And protruding some above the

Snow. He sits in his study
And thinks of the green of May
And red of June. He awaits

The return of his daughter and
The start of his dinner,
Hearty, he hopes, and hot. He

Dreams the sound of her feet
Upon the stairs, but realizes
That if he has fallen asleep he

Is now awake for she has entered
His room. He smiles,
Stretches forth his hands,

Hands that she steps forward and
Holds. He remembers how
He used to write to her mother

When he went to such distant places
As Greensboro and Elsie stayed
Here at home to guard the fort,

As they used to joke. Holly pulls
Slightly and he stands, shaky
At first, yet, recalling

The hikes he took last spring.

Wallace Stevens Welcomes Doctor Jung into Heaven

"Doggone, they've let you in at last, Doc! Gee,
I'm real *glad.*" And indicated angels puffing horns
Rococo with praise and bray and bray,
And proffered to him saffron ice cream cones
Topped up with glacé cherries and chopped cashew nuts.
"Ach! Horn of Plenty," the good Doctor said.

So Long? Stevens
(Dream Song 219)

He lifted up, among the actuaries,
a grandee crow. Ah ha & he crowed good.
That funny money-man.
Mutter we all must as well as we can.
He mutter spiffy. He make wonder Henry's
wits, though, with an odd

. . . something . . . something . . . not there in his flourishing art.
O veteran of death, you will not mind
a counter-mutter.
What was it missing, then, at the man's heart
so that he does not wound? It is our kind
to wound, as well as utter

a fact of happy world. That metaphysics
he hefted up until we could not breathe
the physics. *On our side,*
monotonous (or ever-fresh) — it sticks
in Henry's throat to judge — brilliant, he seethe;
better than us; less wide.

Wallace Stevens' Letters

Wallace Stevens comes hurrying down from the mountain, calling for more tea.
He is stern this man whom I love,
Doubtful of the rocks on which he sits.
If the gods are all dead, then he should be mean. . . .
And when he approaches, garden petals fall.
He walks, he thinks of god, he walks.
The terrible aging is over! The handsome dancer
Hurries in, stiff and stern and almost like a hero.

Against Biography

We came to where the trees, if there were trees,
say, a little group of them, or a house
maybe, something there, whatever it was,
a man standing, someone, it would be clear
enough, sharp at the edges, but everything else
was blurred, all running together or else
moving — sideways, back and forth — or the scale
was wrong, some of the things close by
were smaller than those set farther back, so that though
we saw something, and saw it plain enough,
we saw it nowhere, there wasn't any place
for it to be, or any place for us.
We wandered. Not quite aimless. Man here, though,
would live without biography; it needs
a time and place: there isn't any: who
could say, not smiling, me and my world
or so and so and his time, and stage a play
clothed properly in front of sets,
and believe that this made time and place of the world?

No, we had come too far for that belief
and saw ourselves as ghosts against the real,
and time and place as ghosts; there is the real.
It is there. Where we are: nowhere. It is there.

The Hierophant of Hartford

I.
Never has a noble vocabulary been loved so much:

Bronze, first, and then *procession*, in all its forms,
As in: "The bronze processional of the oaks . . ."

Genius, linked with many nouns, as though the world
Were sentient, a student of experience and time.

Then *summer*, always, that genial season
With its carnivorous clouds and inestimable flowers.

He loved the *sun's* fiery accompaniment and pagan light;
The *sea* gnashing its immense and aqueous teeth.

And he loved to say words more than once,
As in "The sun's bronze genius above the summer sea."

II.
A world needs trees to jungle it, and storied beasts.

The mind's occult menagerie was his:
A polychrome of swans and peacocks, owls and doves.

Golden-eyed macaws made music in the boughs
While cinnamon trees sweetened evening's purple fall.

All this tangled in the mind's vast hinterland
As summer's genius greened the season's blue pavilion.

And in that Paradise of Adams, Badroulbadour appeared,
Gaunt Fernando, silly Crispin and sad Ramon,

Silent interlocutors whose sisters sang as well
Faceless as the sea-bronzed sand where the wind stirred.

III.
The objective world and the mind are separate, but one.

On points of paradox his poems danced.
Such was his conundrum to puzzle in exact verses.

Master of the pure word, sesquipedalia of the sentence,
Palm and hemlock were the efflorescence of his thought,

Feral sea and river his watery amanuenses,
Or he was theirs. Order was an idea posed in equipoise.

Yet the world is empty of our spirit, as we of its,
If spirit it has, known only of Imagination's avatar.

No prayer but the snowman's numb avowels.
No gods but satyrs under the sun's broad bacchanal.

IV.
He was the singer of the intellect's baroque enchantments.

On ordinary evenings he might pause to scry the heavens
Or the solemn houses of Connecticut,

The clapboard sameness of bourgeois habitations
In which inmates, gowned like ghosts, serenely roamed.

Ciscisbeo of Hartford's plain allurements,
A fictive music played across the movement of his lines,

Orchestrations of the greater Vocalissumus
That trembled solely on the spirit with a soundless sound.

O prodigal, soloist of the mind's Reality, the scrawny cry —
The poem's elemental *it*, whatever it its it is.

Thinking of Wallace Stevens

After so many years the familiar
seems even more strange, the hands

one was born with even more remote,
the feet worn to discordant abilities, face fainter.

I love, loved you, Esmeralda, darling Bill.
I liked the ambience of others, the clotted crowds.

Inside it was empty, at best a fountain in winter,
a sense of wasted, drab park, a battered nonentity.

Can I say the whole was my desire?
May I again reiterate my single purpose?

No one can know me better than myself,
whose almost ancient proximity grew soon tedious.

The joy was always to know it was the joy,
to make all acquiesce to one's preeminent premise.

The candle flickers in the quick, shifting wind.
It reads the weather wisely in the opened window.

So it is the dullness of mind one cannot live without,
this place returned to, this place that was never left.

Thirteen Ways of Eradicating Blackbirds

I

Reason with them. Speak softly. Hide your stick.

II

Buy them off. Six tons of feed corn, old wheat
and rusty sorghum ought to do the trick.

III

Drop brochures of Capistrano, complete
with winter rates. Tell them they are swallows.

IV

Frighten their children with authentic stuffed owls.

V

Stand in a field and threaten. Stomp, bellow
like a nincompoop. Point and shout, Pow! Pow!

VI

Declare a park. Hire them to pick up trash.
When they call in sick, relocate the park.

VII

Dye yourself black. Whirl about wildly, thrash,
flap, chirp, and tweet like a demented lark.

VIII

Set out tanks of discount peanut butter.
Verily, it gloms to the roof of their beaks.

IX

Take a million hostages. Then mutter
about one death a day. Ignore their shrieks.

X

Convert the Super Dome to microwave.
Tell them it's a pie. Them dumbbutts can't count.

XI

Build a monstrous runway near their roost. Pave
it with bird brains. Black feather the airport.

XII

Give them to THREE. To TEN. To a THOUSAND.
O. K. Call the Marines. Show the bastards.

XIII

Napalm and flame throw. Douse em in lead.
Waste em. Rack their dark wings. Gas them real dead.
Laser, defoliate, butt stroke and blast.
Pop out each beady, inscrutable eye.
Pound them to soup! Win! Win! Win! Die! Die! Die!

The Sound of Things and Their Motion

All night, the blank page.
All night, the unopened book beat its black wings
against the glass, and I woke, forgetful.

Just like in the movies, the girl is there then gone,
each frame suspended midair.
This moment, wherever it finds us, is neither

mine nor yours.
A place with no
single word rises around

us with the bare
suddenness of a house,
wherein one finds

an unstained coffee mug, a cigarette burned to ash.
An iris rots in a vase above the fireplace.
Which *I* mattered, which earned its belonging?

The nerves, their graceless hum, now quieted.
At times the window and everything in it is blue.
The wish to damage and deny is its own season.

Unless an omen overwhelms the willow,
the pond is dried up and gone and every
proposition forgets the one before it. The camphor field

between grapes and echoes, blazes until its darkening.
Nothing candles the heart so
            much as loss.

Names tell me names to trace
the ways back

towards the saying of some
delicate,
some infinitely stuttering thing.

Easter Service

He half expects a Chinese dragonhead
will bloom from the weave of golden chasuble,
its fangs grinning behind some scalloped fire.
Choir voices surround the lifted chalice,
the elemental dying God wrapped
in music made to storm the sky and purge
the debris of fact. He vaguely sings along.
To his ear it seems a belated howl,
or rude oversimplified foretelling.

Outside the big dome, the rain keeps falling
on shrubs still curtailed, stumped by the slashed
cold air. The unseasonal chill determines
spring's delay; green stuff on its own knows
what to do. The windows, too, are changed.
St. John keeps his shape but the colors cross,
pressing green on red. The lamb's fleece
gleams darkly, the backlight's too unsteady.
The voices run like color down the walls.

On such a morning, he stood on deck and watched
the sullen Azores, not at heaven's distance,
taking the sun while he sailed past. Or:
he held still, the landmass drifted by,
unshadowed, absorbed by such deep brilliance,
as if its body was never actually placed
or brought into the light. Certainly no thought
of God, but maybe earth's rank intelligence,
another holiness, heavy flowers of the sea.

He was the privileged witness, and messenger
to himself, mind to mind, earth's thought thinking.
But if he passed again he'd surely see
a different phase of dark, the littoral shaved
and notched by waves. The new Atlantic swell
would lift him toward the land he thought he knew:
the vegetal islands, flexed in memory,
have become anxious hungry animals,
their voluptuous distance lived in, never crossed.

Newfound robins, redbirds, branches rough
with leaf buds, hedgerows still disclosing
their entanglements, church-organ wail
muted by stone while the sky soon goes
from gray to stunned oceanic green.
But here at Mass there is no history.
The core translation, human and divine,
repeats a million times, each time true,
a fixed thickened everlastingness.

Simpleminded, expectant, a little aroused
by what she's learned, the reverent Mary comes
to find a gorgeous boy slouched by the tomb,
his voice a skein of wind and water. Offhand,
he says that He has risen. Her confusion
worsens with belief. Spread the news.
Tell the others that stone-bound earth,
its molten core, couldn't hold the man God.
Tell them they will never die again.

Incense drenches the air, a smoky figure
of praise designing the high old trace,
then gone. Then more, again. He tells himself
he cannot die, and his insistent hoot,

aggrieved angel-noise, reminds him that belief
isn't knowledge. Desire becomes unfleshed,
intelligence a fulsome ghost, or dream,
and he feels the gravity of life lift
in music's praiseful vaporous dance.

But there was also unnerved January.
The sun at 7 A.M., a dragonhead
above the lake, an ungrieved liquid sun
smarting the lakeside snowdump mounds that smoked
as if the seasonal thaw had really come.
The new light scorched the icebound fields
and picked up millions of silvered points
washing down the street to meet him. Or not meet him.
He walked east anyway, to enter that place,

as if creation, while it comes undone,
could tell him what was there beyond all this.
Unrecorded stars, the happy chaos cry
of galaxies, other voices he might hear
and yet not understand. That's what he knows
of heaven. And all. That's the angry crossing
to the mind outside his own. It's what he hears
in the infinite covered space stuffed with song
that curves, unsettled, inside his desperate ear.

Crispin's Theory

Tiny islands spice the harbor,
the smallest mere huddles of bedrock,
the largest a dozen acres
of saplings stunted by wind.

We dock at the lone inhabited
point, a spine of houses and shops
so narrow the inhabitants share
front yards, and the general store

extends on pilings on both shores
of the spit at the northern tip.
Ramshackle houses, half abandoned,
hold their ground. Indians live here,

digging clams, fishing, motorboating
to the city for construction jobs.
A gaggle of black-haired young men
smiles and shakes our hands. One of them,

inflamed by invisible forces,
calls me by name. He's an artist,
and wants to show off his paintings.
In a loft facing the city,

a distant misty construct
bobbing on the oily chop,
he wields canvases as star-struck
as Van Gogh's. I want to name this

young man's genius after someone else
and assuage my dread of origins,
but the paint's too thick and kinetic,
and the color's too personal.

He has shown them in the galleries,
but when a pop singer bought one
because it complemented her clothes,
he kept the rest for himself.

We have to return to the mainland.
Motoring back past brittle islands
groping like swimmers for breath,
I decide to walk on water

and inspire impossible works
of art, the kind no one can buy,
and bring them to that island town.
I'd prop them against every house

and walk the young men up and down
and let them breathe the rich excrescence
for lack of which the large world suffers
in secret, requiring sea-wind

and thousands of miles of whitecaps
to brace the human effort
and lend it the pure dialectic
of an opposing natural force.

Poem of This Climate

The heads of those peonies sway
slightly in the late afternoon
light — deeply red
blurs floating in a slanting corner
of the yard. One single iris
rises there, its manifold face
open for anyone to see.

In my heart's backwardness
the women I've thought loveliest
have been a little dowdy
and pinched around their eyes,
faces entirely without
guile, though a little too long
or too round. They have
swayed me beyond measure
in uneven light.

The perfectly pretty — those
with nothing ungainly
to conceal — need no unbuttoning;
they must regret nothing. Everything
is already there to be seen:
slim irises rising
among awkward peonies.

In rooms reached by sagging stairs
in renovated houses,

I talked half the night.
The reluctantly unhooked dresses
and loosened breasts
were not some little prize,
but the empirical kiss
the world sometimes relinquishes.

So I believe in love, though
less now than before — I have stood
before mirrors as uneven
as a lake's windswept surface,
and bathed in the amber
light glinting from figurines
and bottles of cologne
while from their beds with flowered
sheets (covered
with dusty sleeping bags)
they have fixed me
with contracted irises, knowing me
superfluous
to the deepest purposes
but necessary, too, like a Christian
angel, an agent of some Will
greater than the future
tense. I have felt the light
shift, as if a storm had passed
at dawn, leaving the sky perfectly clear
and set with only a few shreds
of white cloud like discarded clothing.

The pure peonies sway
in light so perfectly uttered
it cannot be countenanced

and the intricately sexual
parsings of a robin's song
drift through the open window
on the white air of morning.

Variation on a Theme by Stevens

In fall and whiskey weather when
the eye clears with the air and blood
comes up to surface one last time
before the winter and its sleeps,
the weeds go down to straws,
the north wind strips most birds
out of the atmosphere and they
go southward with the sunlight,
the retired people, and rich airs.
All appetites revive and love
is possible again in clarity
without the sweats of heat: it makes
warmth. The walleyed arctic birds
arrive to summer in the fall,
warmed by these chills; geese
practice their noisy Vs,
half a horizon wide, and white owls
hide from their crows in the pines.
Therefore it is not tragic to stay
and not tragic or comic to go,
but it is absolutely typical to say
goodbye while saying hello.

Son and Poet

He lay on white sand,
a boy and a man,
waited for god
to rise from the surf
and expiate all
his Protean shifts,

his infinite self
like infinite stars.

Constellations eluded
what scenes he imagined,
sage faces, brave heroes
night rendered eternal;

one glowed in another
until he saw none.

In surf, slow erasure
of time sounded easy,
easy, and eased him
asleep and awash

in ancestral light.

At the Canoe Club

(*to Wallace Stevens*)

Just a short time ago I sat with him,
Our arms were big, the heat was on,
A glass in hand was worth all tradition.

Outside the summer porch the viable river
Defied the murmurations of guile-subtle
Truths, when arms were bare, when heat was on,

Perceptible as picture: no canoe was seen.
Such talk, and such fine summer ease,
Our heart-life against time's king backdrop,

Makes truth the best perplexity of all,
A jaunty tone, a task of banter, rills
In mind, an opulence agreed upon,

Just so the time, bare-armed and sultry,
Suspend its victims in illusion's colors,
And subtle rapture of a postponed power.

The Voice of Wallace Stevens

is like a planet —
irrefutable in its trajectory —

with the *ancient accent* of a Cicero
as played by Charles Laughton
with a touch of Ray Milland.

Unhurried, he allows each word
to inhale its proper air,

making of shadows something substantial
as teak or mahogany
furniture in a businessman's den.

While conversely what is real
(and he raises the question often)
is polished to an invisible gleam.

When he says: *There it was word for word,*
The poem that took the place of a mountain

he is not speaking figuratively.

The mountain left. The poem stayed.
You can count on it to remain like that.

The Refuge

The winter is made and you have to bear it
— Wallace Stevens, "The Dwarf"

A leaf floats toward the island,
to a grove of winter trees,
naked branches curling toward the sky —
a small island with a bed of fronds.

Things come back aged, leaves pushed
by currents, grayed —
faces changed by time.

On my way through my old town, I meet
my Greek professor.
Diana? Eyes fixed on me, she whispers,
        cos' è successo!
            what happened!

My island on the Adriatic has
rocks bulging in all directions, to meet
rains or sun,
rocks that hide time passing.

Those massive stones shaped
in extravagant turrets, moats, are
repository of my past. They will honor
an ancient promise of asylum
to a tarnished leaf.

To my poor semblance
of the young woman they remember,
they will offer a couch of leaves
to spend the night.

A Woman on the Beach

for Wallace Stevens

As if they grew in fields that sang unploughed
into her hands, she plants the rocking waves,
tooled with phantoms over shale, with long
unrooting waverings that climb the night.

She'd cliff and order them or at least their light
if they splashed toward her touch, or curling in
with human toes warmed toward the welcome shore —
but she the shore, she the shore, stands clear,

and doesn't order them, since they won't hear;
and after tides, she follows clouds,
planting out and harvesting in, racking
the waves with the harvests in, to cloud

the ocean's green with seedlings gathered
dark from dizzy, like no bounded dream.
The waves don't hold her where they haven't been.

At the Casa Marina

I don't understand the genius of the sea, just a squandering
of waves over rock, sand, bits of broken shell.
The railroad baron who built this hotel is long dead,
but under management of the Marriott Corporation, his hotel,
with its wrap-around veranda, is still grand — the brochures
didn't lie. All afternoon under the dispassionate rage of the sun,
we laze on chaises, now made of plastic and not wood,
where years ago you'd have lounged, almost fully-dressed,
a proper and decorous late Victorian. The world has changed —
though certainty of change is a kind of constancy, after all.
And since your old friend Ramon Fernandez, too, is dead,
to you I'll pose my questions: Does it make you unhappy
to know whole civilizations of coral are dying around these islands?
Do the dead care that they're pulling down the conch houses
to build condos? — do you even know what that last word means?
Only 90 miles from Cuba, sometimes at these resorts
half-eaten bodies will wash up. Those shoddy rafts, lashed
together inner tubes coming apart in open water.
It's not capitalism or the fine weather that brings them here,
they're just hungry, and maybe a little ambitious,
desirous of a better life. Refined as you are, you probably
have a painting in mind — Homer's *The Gulf Stream*,
perhaps — musing that the shark is hunger incarnate.
But it's all crueler than any concept or irony you might conceive.
At sunset, an offshore breeze tousles the palms, on a reach
a catamaran moves fast and easy over swells and whitecaps.
It's so goddamn beautiful, the failing light making too many colors
to name, seen for a moment then lost among the rods
and cones of the retina, the myriad firings of nerve endings,

with the brain's numb wonder hardly catching up.
Year after year you came back, to this beach in Key West
where pelicans fall from the sky, slamming into the surf,
stunning the small fish, taking them up in great, mad gulps.
I'm not certain exactly what it was you loved about this place,
though when I listen hard I can hear that strange singing,
which might be the crying out of those drowned Haitians
and Cubans, or only the sand grinding under the tide,
echoing in the sad shell of my ear, whispering some nonsense
about the eternal, an oceanic ache transcending the ages.

from "The Hugeness of That Which Is Missing"

Contact

Call the direction the eye is looking
the line of sight. There
where it grazes the surface
         of the visibly surging
without reference to a field of human presence,
don't look away.

            I haven't looked away.

The neurons spike quickly. And the catastrophe
will be consummated even to the end, to the absence of ambiguity,
a new range of feeling. Torn awake. What if
a man went into his house and leaned his hand
against the wall and the wall
         was not?

Look how your relation to truth creates a tension
you have slackened with compromise.
         Yes, and the more
distant it is, the more I have valued it. But to stand
where the crossing happens, as fall oaks fold
         into lake light, and so
wearing reflection, take a further step inside —

         No, the voice said, you will strike out
into a forest of pain, unpathed, wolved, clouds muffling the mountain ridge
         and spilling down in runnels,

blindness with confusion come to parle, at variance with,
measuring out an exile between self and self. Driven
transverse. Nevertheless you will begin to arrive, to know
                                        from intimate impulse
the crucial experience of . . . the threat of dissolution of . . . but not yet.
There is something more
                        than rhythms of distance and presence,
of more quality than the set of qualities determining figure and ground
and suffering, where respite is so often
misinterpreted as a horizon.

Isn't the word for a turn of phrase
itself a turn of phrase?
                Something was given to me as a present
and a specter was attached to me, pregnant
                                        with equivocation.

And in the throat of language,
and in the early June riots of starlings,
and in some crumbs in the seam of a book,
the solid real steps out from infinitely diluted experience
saying, *Tongue I gave you. Eyes.*

At any point in the trajectory, the body might stop. Do you recall this part?

But who is it that is speaking
in the glorious, unstrung light?

Wallace Stevens, I think of you

Every time I pass Hartford on I-91,
with its high-rise glittering buildings,
temples to glass and steel,
all those insurance drones
sitting in cubicles
measuring out their lives
bent over figures
and paper,

I think of you,
your glorious, opulent mind,
confined each day
for so many years
in sterile ugliness.

No wonder in odd moments
and each evening
you traveled
the byways of language,
the wild, flying imagery.
In poems perfectly formed,
polished and smooth,
you found

the poems that not only suffice
but bloom like perfect orchids
carved
out of that pink marble
that still glows
even years after
you put down your pen.

Money

Money is a kind of poetry.
— Wallace Stevens

Money, the long green,
cash, stash, rhino, jack
or just plain dough.

Chock it up, fork it over,
shell it out. Watch it
burn holes through pockets.

To be made of it! To have it
to burn! Greenbacks, double eagles,
megabucks and Ginnie Maes.

It greases the palm, feathers a nest,
holds heads above water,
makes both ends meet.

Money breeds money.
Gathering interest, compounding daily.
Always in circulation.

Money. You don't know where it's been,
but you put it where your mouth is.
And it talks.

Saturday and Its Festooned Potential

Faces unlike weather
never return
no matter how closely
they resemble rain

In this theater, time
isn't cruel, just different

Does that help?

When the overgrown skyway
becomes calm
humans get quiet

When the notions of myth
or collective anything
is undone by wind chimes
by a gentle tink tink

When the mind is opened forth
by gentle tink tink
or light speckled
and whooping in the periphery

When light whooping
and speckled is most pleasing
to a body at rest

When thought, open
attaches itself to repose
to the forehead

When twigs swaying
just outside
the library's large glass
signal, scratch, and join
to an idea of history

When twigs scratching
join to an idea of time
to a picture of being

Like to be beside and becoming
to be another and oneself
to be complete inside the poem

To be oneself becoming a poem

At the Grave of Wallace Stevens

(Section 14, Cedar Hill Cemetery, Hartford, Connecticut)

1

One thinks of the gods dissolving in mid-air
And the towering stillness of a cathedral at dawn.

One thinks of a solitary reader closing his book
In a ring of lamplight puddled on the desk.

Wind ruffles the curtains all night long
And the music of the spheres is silence.

Raindrops break the watery skin of ponds
And ponds are shattered mirrors of the absolute.

Stars are the white tears of nothingness.
Nothingness grieves over the disintegrating gods.

2

One imagines him as a prodigious morning walker
And a lonely metaphysician pausing in the park,

A rose rabbi, a sturdy man on a wide path
Dreaming of a sky washed clean by doubt.

One pictures him strolling under the umbrella
Pines and buttonwoods on the way to work,

Imagination's largest thinker conjuring up
Songs of human radiance twanging in the mist.

One thinks of him by the lake in a hard rain:
Mirrors on mirrors mirroring the emptiness.

                              3
We have stepped out into a summer storm:
Mute thunder and luminescent air, a wishbone

Of lightning turned upside down in the clouds,
A crescent of light poised on a dark steeple.

We have scattered sprigs of holly on the grave
And noticed the rosebushes blooming in shadows.

But we have not knelt at the heavy slab
Of Rhode Island granite carved with dates.

The ambassador of imagination is dead
And the guitars are silent. So farewell

                              4
To the maker of mournful summer melodies,
The connoisseur of moonlight, improvisation's king.

Farewell to the laudator of imperfection,
Grandeur in a business suit, the stylist

Of the void. Farewell to dried fruit
From California, tea imported from Ceylon,

And fresh ideas sailing in from anywhere.
Farewell to fidelity bonds and surety claims.

All those worldly realms of reflection
Have been traded in for a slope of trees.

5

The graveyard is carved into separate parts:
Streams and ponds, muddy paths, curving lanes.

You taught us to imagine the sublime
In a bare place, filling in the spaces.

Thus the sky is a lake brimming with tears,
The lake is a cloudy mirror. All morning

The wind rises and falls on transparent wings
And the traffic winding along Asylum Avenue

Is like a ghostly procession, a cortege!
The domes of skyscrapers gleam in the distance.

Asylum Avenue

Here is a region through which you move, yet which moves
through you as you make your *paseo*; it is as if it were receptive to
the space you bring along with you, and as if all the spaces flowed
into each other like clear, green water. It is itself a wide walk past
heavily meaningless cars and their motion, descending in curving
and gracious declines into the business of being a street. Yet it
never needs to become a mere boulevard, broadly proclaiming
itself over buried and forgotten bulwarks, but remains the
extension of what it comes toward, which itself kindly advances to
meet what has been moving forward at it for so very long. It is
the neighborhood of points of refuge through which you pass: they
continually astonish you with their inventiveness, with the
manner in which food and drink have been tucked away in them,
with the devices by which you may see and not be seen. And
suppose that there was an encounter to be had there (I think of a
recently dead friend appearing at your door, his arms full of books
and papers, in place of someone else you had invited, cheerfully
assuring you that the reports of his sudden death in Italy were
quite mistaken)— it would be as much part of your walk as your
very setting out. It would not be occasional. Nor would the
sidewalk along the asphalt shore constitute a road. It would be
a way of getting to work.

from "Even in Paris"

to the Memory of L. Donald Maher, 1921–1966

II
Dear Roderick, the New Year has set in —
like an epidemic. The wolves are gone,
but Villon has the winter down *patte bas*!

Christmas *is* a deadly season here,
illustrating the old Parisian rule:
every silver lining is tarnished by clouds.

Life seems so piecemeal: "Oh that, that belongs
to my Litter Period." So much for '52.
Perhaps just sending this, or anything,

to Schenectady will make the pieces fit.
News — not mine, but *the* news, Roderick,
leaves me at a loss for language, clogged

like a bottle of Burgundy held upside down.
Guess what! Paris is being visited
(*graced* is hardly the word) by Crispin himself!

who never once in seventy years detoured
farther out of territorial
waters than a weekend in Key West.

Remember Edna's story about Henry James
preferring to stay among the vegetables
when she took him with her to Les Halles —

"precisely because their organs of increase
are not so prominent" . . . Was Europe's meat
too bloody for my poet all these years?

Yet there he sat, the old Comedian,
continuous as an eggshell, right beside
Ivo, and freezing like the rest of us

— only from higher motives, I am sure —
in Sainte Chapelle, contingency resolved
to kingliness. Each time I tried to make

acknowledgments, the Poulenc interfered,
as well as Ivo's scowling all the while,
like a Dying Swan that is very, very cross.

"The kings sit down to music, and the queens"
— to alter Kipling's verse —"stand up to dance,"
by which I mean that Ivo ran away

once I informed him who our neighbor was . . .
Another *fine*, another *fin-de-siècle*
feast or fast with dying dowagers:

the past is always Ivo's choice because
it is drained of fear. I braved the present out,
putting the usual impertinences as

to When and Where and Does the prospect please,
and Will you go on to visit Italy?
("I think not. Italians are only the French

in a good mood.") At least I got replies!
"The tourist's purpose is to be delighted.
Nothing odd or obscure. I have survived

too long on postcards from Paris or Toulon.
At my age, I may say, life melts in the hand,
and I have dined enough with the faithful dead."

Timid yet tenacious, I asked on —
they must have been the questions he could use;
he did not turn away, yet seemed to exude

a gentleness no longer incarnate but somehow
hovering above him in a nimbus, even though
the light in Sainte Chapelle was going dim . . .

Roderick, I was gossiping with a god!
Maybe because I showed I knew as much
without an autograph or a lock of hair,

I was told I might escort him — *steer*, he said —
to the Louvre next day. ("What I want to see
is in the Orangerie: is that the Louvre too?")

In order to make "sense" of the *Nymphéas* . . .
"I have been told one is embraced, they curve
around one in a continuous ecstasy . . .

It seems worth leaving even Hartford for that.
I have always wanted to stand inside the light
which falls at home — falls out, falls down: falls,

that is the point. In Hartford, the light falls,
and what is fallen does not cease to fall.
I'd like to let those water-lilies have

their way with me; I'd like to learn from them:
if Anything could be explained, then Everything
would be explained . . ." There was, of course, a catch!

No one's to know he ever came here — no
first impressions of Paris, photographs
of boulevard encounters, above all

no poems. The whole preposterous episode
is to be wiped out, elided — *never was*!
I made a stab: "And have you come with Mrs. . . . ?"

"No. Journeys taken together lead to hell.
I want to be, this once, a living man
and a posthumous artist. Ideal. Shall we, then?"

Surely this was He-Mannerism at its best,
an invitation being the sincerest form
of flattery; besides, it was a mere *traipse*

squiring the old absquatulator home
to his safe haven in — where else? — the Ritz!
Even incognito our Crispin knows his place.

We talked, or he — dialogue being no more
than a literary fiction taken for a fact
of life — *he* talked, in a timbre bearing words

before him on a salver: "Limelight is bad.
What's best for me is half-light . . . *crépuscule?*
La lumière qui tombe entre deux tabourets:

the profit of French is how readily it submits
to prose. I suppose I am one of those [three rhymes!]
who can tell you at dusk what others deny by day."

By now we had advanced to the Place Vendôme
where the Column bedevils what it can't adorn
and where, at the wicked doorway of the Ritz,

the din of inequity swallowed up my man
as if there were no such still pond as poets!
The night remained. How sad it is to part

from people we've known only a little while!
Hours to pass, to pass through, to pass by . . .
I stopped at the Reine. Ivo of course had flown

that brazen coop which would display till dawn
a nature shocking-pink in tooth and claw . . .
Not much rest tonight. The rest anon.

Well, dear, we reached the *empty* Orangerie
(day-after-Christmas void) and there we stood,
enveloped by the ovals of nenuphars

— yes, rather *like* the islands of Langerhans,
actually: there *is* an anatomical sense
of visceral perspectives. Once inside,

you must admit, a cycle of mustard and mauve
makes it hard to link how much there is *of* it
to how little there is *to* it. Roderick,

do you know what a *temenos* is? A ring of dread,
the invulnerable range the Greeks proposed
around their gods and heroes. That's what I saw:

my poet paralyzed by the perimeter
of a wave without horizon, without shore . . .
He stood stock still, and I think it was awe

he felt at how the visual could turn
visionary. He stayed there a long while
(I, meantime, loaded up on postcards: X

marks where he stood, admonished by Monet.)
"We also ascend dazzling," is all he said,
or all I could make out — is it a quote?

You'd have thought I had *awakened* him
by shouting in his ear; he started up
when I *whispered* was he happy? "Happy here?

— how hideous the happiness one wants,
how beautiful the misery one has! . . .
I think I'll stay a little longer here.

Alone." I left him then, of course —
mine was the backward glance of Orpheus
or of Lot's Wife, the unretarding gaze

that loses the beloved where last seen:
my Sacred Monster loomed, one big black lump
in a circle of besieging light, and Rod,

he was slowly, in a sort of demonic shuffle,
turning, turning round the oval room,
palms out and humming harshly to himself —

it was, I could tell, a ritual exploit
danced by the world's most deliberate dervish — not
whirling but centripetal. Outside

the air was crumbling, there was no more sky —
only that Paris substitute which fills
the calendar till spring. Ivo won't know

what he incanted like a sacred text:
"We also ascend dazzling." All Ivo knows
is Rumanian nursery rhymes and the Almanach

da Gotha, which he keeps in his medicine chest.
Roderick, do you recognize the phrase?
Myself, I think — however insane I may be —

it does console one to have living gods
on whose warm altars one can lay one's wreath,
as I have done — I brought him there, after all.

Dear Roderick, if you have been denied
such aptitudes of worship, I pity you.
But enough about you, dear, let me return

to my distances, my deference: the great
are like high mountains, you must be
away from them to enjoy them properly.

I'd better stop before I've told it all —
some people can tell all before they start;
suppose you try, dear.

                    Happy New Year,

                              Richard

from "118 Westerly Terrace"

His alter ego *"walked"*—

Henry James

In the house the house is all
house and each of its authors
passing from room to room

Short eclogues as one might
say on tiptoe do not infringe

I want my own house I'm
you and you're the author
You're not all right you're

all otherwise it appears as
if you don't care who you
are — if you count the host

Don't worry I go with the
house your living's where
you walk or have walked

I'd rather read than hurt a
hair of you listen to me

Premeditated twilight this
house a nearest wrapped
bundle of belonging idle

Slip back through grasses
dabble our bare feet in

Poets have imagined you
whoever you are implicit
melody familiar metaphor

bawdy tapestries archaic
pillage love patience the
scales the dogs the boots

Lieutenant-of-the-reserve
voice then scraps of tunes
and the scraping of chairs

Walk under paper lantern
nothing secretarial about
this paper house on paper

After a Cryptic and Bitter Exchange

with Elsie, I imagine Stevens takes
the Pierce Arrow out for a ride, his face
ghostly in the dashboard's glow. The car

weaves around the pleadings of peepers,
past mudflats and marshes. The running
boards rattle, the tires thrum-a-thrum.

Perhaps, through spring's high lavender
dusk, he drives the river road from Hartford
to Higganum and back, through the flooded

washbasins of swans and old heron haunts,
under the lofty estates of sun-bled clouds,
stopping now and then to catch the chat of bird

parvenus from the South, his rage
dissipating as tropes arrange themselves
in the convolute concupiscence of his

cortex's curly folds. He must realize
he is among the loneliest poets on Earth,
least-desired by her he desired most.

Erotic, sensuous, repressed, yet self-
possessed in the grandeur of his solitude,
in the hepatica fields of his thought,

he chases his sense of things in a gaiety
of sounds. I see him roadside, standing
beside his cooling car, transfixed in

last light ripped from essential winds,
consoling himself once more with the idea
of his interior paramour, the one who,

sans nuance, sans parle-vous, sans capricious
cavortings of vowels, he cannot conceive . . .
his mademoiselle of vast endowments.

The Pattern-Parallel Map or Graph

The sky? — ultramarine, tinted black, lines
of black ink. Newspapers, mud, fishtails,
betel nuts, trampled on along Canal Street.

Luck turns out hot. Eros is extraordinarily
lucky to have found Psyche. According
to the story, which is taken from Apuleius,
Eros's and Psyche's bodies are wet and hot.

Nine years — where does that take us
on the pattern-parallel map or graph?
Nine years from two thousand — nineteen ninety-one . . .
Wallace Stevens — him again —
in his commonplace book,
an entry made in nineteen thirty-four:
"Ananke is necessity or fate personified,
the saeva Necessitas of Horace
Odes Book I No. 35, to Fortune . . ."

I'm the one who hears it. Chromatically
suspended, as the notes feel their way
from intervals to motifs, a progression
in a manner that disguises the key —
a linear polyphony forming harmonies in strange
developments. All kinds of different stuff, mixed
and fused, is where it's at, chunks of vibrato . . .
Simultaneity requires the use of a topological
logic. Time compressed — interactivity escalated
to maximum speed. Why not? Have their official

status changed from human to animal, they live like
animals already. Once they've attained animal status
dozens of groups will come forward to defend them.
What, let's say, in twelve years
will the zone of suffering that exists
outside the established orders look like? There's
Venus again, moving across the sun,
in a mini-eclipse visible twice every century or so.
There's the achieved conception, a God
accessible and inaccessible, merciful
and just, human and divine, completed
not far from the Black Sea. That mood,
intensely subjective, scenes and myths
reemerged. There, on the table, a flower the yellow
of flax closes, the irises unfolding,
two of them deep blue-purple, a third is larger,
and china blue. There, small, bright birds
in wooden cages in a store on East Broadway,
an illuminated scroll unrolled on the counter.

After a Phrase Abandoned by Wallace Stevens

The alp at the end of the street
— Stevens' Notebooks

The alp at the end of the street
Occurs in the dreams of the town.
Over burgher and shopkeeper,
Massive, he broods,
A snowy-headed father
Upon whose knees his children
No longer climb;
Or is reflected
In the cool, unruffled lakes of
Their minds, at evening,
After their day in the shops,
As shadow only, shapeless
As a wind that has stopped blowing.

Grandeur, it seems,
Comes down to this in the end —
A street of shops
With white shutters
Open for business . . .

from "A Stone Wall in Providence"

for Mary Caponegro

1

At dawn the sun investigates the blue copper dome
of the Christian Science church and at nightfall

the same formal acorn inhibits the roseate light.
Then it is dark. It is winter. The long propositions

of romance, as much a part of us as cracks in glaze
are part of porcelain, become hard to see in this light.

Hard to hear. The heart is always an investigation.
Let me draw inferences from difficulty. What is hard

is always beginning and comes to an end no more
than the pattern on the scarlet Bokhara carpet does

though it meets its ornamental border and resumes
all the alternative directions its mystery is heir to

thing after thing. So that is what it is: a city new
with fresh air, streets starting to be familiar,

shapes of people always familiar but the air of them, the style
tells me I am in this place, a hope of its own,

grace of its own. Isolate in openness, in the hope of change,
old me in a new city, selfish as colors.

2

A town where streets live up to their names is heavy
like reading a book that takes itself seriously, aesthetics,

grammar, politics. In this town I'm quizzical about my own
name, destiny, reputation. I am a part . . . yes, of that power

that stands to kiss the good and shapes the will instead.
Under the porcelain crucifix the light is keen, candlestick,

milk glass, the imputation of innocence because our eyes
do not analyze the surface deep enough. There is always more

and to such amplitude the simplisms of morality do not reach.
Dare not. What is done in the Mass! How dare the man the wine

the bread the haughty differences make identical! How dare we
be so confused? To bring to one bed so many women as if

never even changing the bright sheets or if they washed themselves
a city! That is how it is, the integrals of danger. I love you

becomes a manifesto, even a theology. Be multiplicitous and prophesy:
the world is one we know so many of by virtue of this quivering I.

3

About that power: it is the serum of questioning
that flows through the blood of the mind. The mind is current

through all flesh, it is a river, it is this river,
slaty pewter, sluggish under the arches at Fox Point

slowly getting around to be sea. The mind is its occasions,
faithful to the cloth and to the swell of hip

that minds the cloth. It is not nowhere. Cleverness of water
to pry everywhere is also its cunning. It can freeze a season

but there is always spring. The dome comes back at morning
far beyond the huge playing field where the girls at hockey

trot with cold red knees under plaid skirts with civil squeals.
And the mind has something to work with again, weary

of the ulcerating languages of night it gnaws at, strange grammar
whereby three A.M. turns into sleep and sleep into dawn

like one long sentence in whateverese.

                4
Like so many codes it is mediated by a wall, an arduous
separation between the world and the world. There they play

and in its hither shade a pair of lovers lies down (or one
lies down and one kneels over) on this suddenly hot day

and beyond them and unseen by them in their slow parade
(he presses her belly lightly with one hand) the field

is full of summery english grass, hurdles, goals, foul lines
and no people. He stands now, she lies, the shadow

would be too cold for me but I am made of it, complected
of its sinister night body here in the high autumn afternoon.

I think they have lain down in me. Whatever they think of
is what I must say — I don't have to say *I* any more, every item

and every relation cannot fail to speak my dialect of mind.
And they go through their own morphologies, lovers, friends,

bodies making comfort for each other in what privacy they find.
They do what lovers do. For instance they are gone.

                    5
There is a wall we walk along to come home. Finding way.
The thing you see, the yellowing young oak, promises to be there,

promises a presentness, indexes a past a whole myth of causation
— acorn — gardener — weather — nurture — light, and as wind fusses it

argues a future in which it will govern a whole range of meanings.
For instance: that tree, do you remember that, by the old wall,

the way it looked, when the field suddenly filled with baseball
and the tree did not change, symbol of great Jupiter, the power

of being about what is on your mind unswervingly. This tree
is my authority. What we need to answer is what asks.

What I need to marry is what comes along. A thing is time.
A thing is a momentary rest between unending contradictions

that intersect in it, cross over each upon other, and regress
into the two directions of our fancy. Thing stays. Times goes, comes.

The Waterbury Cross

Fall. You're driving 84 southwest —
A hillock scarlet as a side of beef
Accosts your eyes. Gigantic on its crest,
An outstretched cross stands waiting for its thief.

Your fingers as though hammered to the wheel
Clench hard. Frost-kindled sumac blazes down
Like true gore pouring from a bogus crown.
The earth grows drizzled, and bedrenched.

Did even Wallace Stevens at the last,
Having sown all his philosophe's wild oats,
Gape for the sacred wafer and clutch fast
To Mother Church's swaddling petticoats?

Connecticut's conversions stun. Is there
Still a wan Christ who clings to hope for me,
Who bides time in a cloud? Choking, my car
Walks over water, across to Danbury.

Modernists on the Grass

Wallace Stevens & Gertrude Stein
were sharing a picnic lunch
a blanket of shredded texts
spread on the grave of Robert Frost
as they discussed insurance
art
& rates of interest
& how to arrange language
so as to elude auditors & invent annuities
paying off ever after
in ambiguity

Annotation

Even accidents falter. The room behind the room
Has lost its particularity, a tent
In a field of tents.
These are like the endings of words
As rooms resemble the beginnings.
Will she choose? As between metal and cloth,
Duration over flexibility, easy handling, touch?
She lay in the brown October grass under an imported sky.
Or, standing inside, she gazes out at the real thing
Shifting behind glass.
To say sky in the face of sky
Is a failure of duration;
The sky escapes.
                  The suburbs are plain,
Especially in winter, if to be plain
Is to be similar. But this
Harbors difference in its midst.
Eventually it will become
The fabulous plaintiff absurdly jeweled,
A city ready to explore
All the oblique ruins of the unsaid.
The unhealed voices soar
Into the predawn like accelerating notes
In a choral mood. All night, she
Hears them, and turns away, and hears again
The refrain of the unspeakable rhyme
And wakes to first light spelling its shield.

The Winter Palace

after Stevens

Above the winter palace of the presidents
A president of presidents prevails,
A blacksmith's hammer in a world of nails.

The perquisites of power are hard by:
Audits for enemies, wiretaps for *Untermen*;
He forgets more than he lets come into ken.

Watch as he whistles up his replicant
Like some gift pup, some checkered spaniel
On no leash but the itch to do his will.

Prisoner by prisoner, his appetites distend
Until he's swallowed Poland in strange tortuous forms,
His eye blind in the center of bright storms.

But when the midnight legislatures meet
He sleeps his ancient sleep and puffs his jowls
Before a conference committee made of owls.

He is content to let a poppet make the news.
Propping up the hapless emperor of guffaws
He abides inside his white house, signing laws.

In a World without Heaven

1.

The youngest feels the winter stars receding
As willows raise their skirts and wave good-bye.

She sings herself a lullaby, mimicking
Her sisters' voices until the room is scoured
Of its emptiness.
                        Each night they kissed
Her forehead and unclenched her fists —
Still clinging to the treasure of the day,
Before they fumbled with the light and closed the door.

2.

Time was the sisters swept the floor more neatly
Than their mother had. They strained with rags
Until the window shone more brightly than the moon.

When the youngest cried at night, cried harder
Than they'd cried themselves when she was born,
They stood on ladders, memorized the view
And brought it home.
                        Soon anything they found
Became a gift. As their collection grew
The room became more cluttered than the world.

3.

One night the youngest heard them rise, one voice
Gathering from their bodies as they wept
For little things they'd have to leave behind.

Willows shivered in the wind that swept
The voice beyond the highway's ribbon of stars.
No one could stop.
                          No one could listen
For the youngest who, once they were gone,
Would have to live alone the longest time.

4.
And when she asked about their bodies, sinking
In the ground, the sisters told her of
A mother, larger than their own, who lifts
Them up and teaches them to wave good-bye:

Children bending plump, unpracticed fingers,
Growing younger, smiling sleepily, forgetting
Every face they'd ever loved. The sisters
Didn't believe the story.
                          Nor did she.
The youngest still remembers how
Their bodies felt against her, damp and warm.

5.
The youngest feels days accumulate
Like objects in the room. Days cut and stacked
Like wood waiting to be burnt to ash
And swept away, ashes soft as feathers
On the floor.
                    There's nobody left to give
Things to. The wood is silent, feathers shine —
A bird still opening its beak as if
To let the singing back inside.
                          Every night
The youngest burns the gifts they left behind.

6.

The room explodes with diamonds in her memory,
A lifetime's worth of fireflies released
From jars where they convinced her they'd died.

But it's only a night like any night, one more
Good-bye, a child rising from the bed
Like a ghost behind the headstone reappearing
To its mother for a final kiss,
                              a butterfly,
Dark lashes against her cheek at last once more
Before we fumble with the light and close the door.

Waking Early Sunday Morning

O to break loose, like the chinook
salmon jumping and falling back,
nosing up to the impossible
stone and bone-crushing waterfall —
raw-jawed, weak-fleshed there, stopped by ten
steps of the roaring ladder, and then
to clear the top on the last try,
alive enough to spawn and die.

Stop, back off. The salmon breaks
water, and now my body wakes
to feel the unpolluted joy
and criminal leisure of a boy —
no rainbow smashing a dry fly
in the white run is free as I,
here squatting like a dragon on
time's hoard before the day's begun!

Vermin run for their unstopped holes;
in some dark nook a fieldmouse rolls
a marble, hours on end, then stops;
the termite in the woodwork sleeps —
listen, the creatures of the night
obsessive, casual, sure of foot,
go on grinding, while the sun's
daily remorseful blackout dawns.

Fierce, fireless mind, running downhill.
Look up and see the harbor fill:

business as usual in eclipse
goes down to the sea in ships —
wake of refuse, dacron rope,
bound for Bermuda or Good Hope,
all bright before the morning watch
the wine-dark hulls of yawl and ketch.

I watch a glass of water wet
with a fine fuzz of icy sweat,
silvery colors touched with sky,
serene in their neutrality —
yet if I shift, or change my mood,
I see some object made of wood,
background behind it of brown grain,
to darken it, but not to stain.

O that the spirit could remain
tinged but untarnished by its strain!
Better dressed and stacking birch,
or lost with the Faithful at Church —
anywhere, but somewhere else!
And now the new electric bells,
clearly chiming, "Faith of our fathers,"
and now the congregation gathers.

O Bible chopped and crucified
in hymns we hear but do not read,
none of the milder subtleties
of grace or art will sweeten these
stiff quatrains shoveled out four-square —
they sing of peace, and preach despair;
yet they gave darkness some control,
and left a loophole for the soul.

No, put old clothes on, and explore
the corners of the woodshed for
its dregs and dreck: tools with no handle,
ten candle-ends not worth a candle,
old lumber banished from the Temple,
damned by Paul's precept and example,
cast from the kingdom, banned in Israel,
the wordless sign, the tinkling cymbal.

When will we see Him face to face?
Each day, He shines through darker glass.
In this small town where everything
is known, I see His vanishing
emblems, His white spire and flag-
pole sticking out above the fog,
like old white china doorknobs, sad,
slight, useless things to calm the mad.

Hammering military splendor,
top-heavy Goliath in full armor —
little redemption in the mass
liquidations of their brass,
elephant and phalanx moving
with the times and still improving,
when the kingdom hit the crash:
a million foreskins stacked like trash . . .

Sing softer! But what if a new
diminuendo brings no true
tenderness, only restlessness,
excess, the hunger for success,
sanity of self-deception
fixed and kicked by reckless caution,

while we listen to the bells —
anywhere, but somewhere else!

O to break loose. All life's grandeur
is something with a girl in summer . . .
elated as the President
girdled by his establishment
this Sunday morning, free to chaff
his own thoughts with his bear-cuffed staff,
swimming nude, unbuttoned, sick
of his ghost-written rhetoric!

No weekends for the gods now. Wars
flicker, earth licks its open sores,
fresh breakage, fresh promotions, chance
assassinations, no advance.
Only man thinning out his kind
sounds through the Sabbath noon, the blind
swipe of the pruner and his knife
busy about the tree of life . . .

Pity the planet, all joy gone
from this sweet volcanic cone;
peace to our children when they fall
in small war on the heels of small
war — until the end of time
to police the earth, a ghost
orbiting forever lost
in our monotonous sublime.

Wallace Stevens Returns from Paris Ruined

Oh for a muse of fire to ascend
the highest heaven of invention.
Everyone at one time or another
calls out for help. A kingdom

for a stage, princes to act, monarchs
(butterflies) to behold a swelling scene.
But then there's King Carlos a.k.a.
Williams down in Jersey, singing

the virtues of his French Father Rasles
among the indigenes of New World Maine,
before he's off for gay Paree
to sing of Tennessee & Boone.

Well, now I have come back, come back
at last, wide-eyed Crispin from across
the seas and Paris gleaned at last: golden
city with water running through her veins

just like Hartford on its hill. Ah, I too
have gone & have returned, a brine-
drenched Crispin, who, having seen it,
is left, alack, without a single song to sing.

No Sop, No Possum, No Jive

We must pit ourselves brutally,
testing the tar and pitch
of immaculate forefathers. Ditto, etc.
X-temporizing, scrounging luxuriously
as we climb intricate cobs, nipples
and rosy vellums inscribed with an oriole.
I see no further than this, though
I've been lower, into hell's orifice;
popped back in like a rabbit!

The Green Eye

Come, child, and with your sunbeam gaze assign
Green to the orchard as a metaphor
For contemplation, seeking to declare
Whether by green you specify the green
Of orchard sunlight, blossom, bark, or leaf,
Or green of an imaginary life.

A mosaic of all possible greens becomes
A premise in your eye, whereby the limes
Are green as limes faintly by midnight known,
As foliage in a thunderstorm, as dreams
Of fruit in barren countries; claims
The orchard as a metaphor of green.

Aware of change as no barometer
You may determine climates at your will;
Spectrums of feeling are accessible
If orchards in the mind will persevere
On their hillsides original with joy.
Enter the orchard differently today:

When here you bring your earliest tragedy,
Your goldfish, upside-down and rigidly
Floating on weeds in the aquarium,
Green is no panorama for your grief
Whose raindrop smile, dissolving and aloof,
Ordains an unusual brightness as you come:

The brightness of a change outside the eye,
A question on the brim of what may be,
Attended by a new, impersonal green.
The goldfish dead where limes hang yellowing
Is metaphor for more incredible things,
Things you shall live among, things seen, things known.

The Noble Rider and the Sound of Words: A Cento

I might be expected to speak of the social,
that is to say sociological or political
obligations of the poet. He has none.
— Wallace Stevens

The soul no longer exists and we droop in our flight.
If only we could yield ourselves to the unreal —
But we cannot yield, we are not free to yield.
Still on the edge of the world in which we live
Is an invincible man, who moves in our midst,
A charioteer traversing vacant space,
Like the empty spirit, smoke-drift of puffed-out heroes,
Or is it perhaps a rider intent on the sun,
Rushing from what is real? It is gorgeous nonsense,
Dear, gorgeous nonsense, the passion of rhetoric.
The enemies of poetry like Freud
Despise the consolation of illusion,
Without which men cannot endure reality,
The cruelty of it. They would have us
Venture into the hostile world, which is,
The way we live and the way we work alike,
A world of ever-enlarging incoherence,
Of violence, the disparagement of reason,
Absent of any authority save force,
The spirit of negation being so active.
We lie in bed and listen to a broadcast,
The drift of incidents, to which we accustom ourselves
As to the weather, the impermanence of the future
And of the past — as for the present,

It is merely an opportunity to repent.
Little of what we believed is true —
Only the prophecies are true:
The movement of people in the intervals of a storm,
A whole generation and a world at war,
And the war only a part of a warlike whole
Beyond our power to tranquilize.
But for the possible poet, the noble rider
Responsive to the most minute demand,
The dead are still living,
Living on the earth or under it,
And what is dead lives with an intensity
Beyond any experience of life —
Black water breaking into reality.
This potent figure cannot be too noble,
The arm of bronze outstretched against all evil.
Don Quixote will make it imperative
For him to choose between the imagination
And brute reality. His choice must be
That they are equal and inseparable.
It is not enough to cover the rock with leaves.
But neither is everything favorable to reality.
The use of that bare word has been enough;
It means something to everyone, so to speak.
Reality is things as they are,
The life that is lived in the scene that it composes,
It is a jungle in itself,
A plainness of plain things, a savagery.
It became violent and so remains,
Wherefore the possible poet must resist
Its pressure, and with the violence within
Protect us from the violence without,
Always in emptiness that would be filled.
One loves and goes back to one's ancient mother

Certainly not as a social obligation
But out of a suasion not to be denied.
Who is it that the poet addresses? Stalin
Might grind his teeth the whole of a Russian winter,
And the poets might be silent in the spring.
Who is it that the poet addresses? A drab?
Or a woman with the hair of a pythoness?
To give life whatever savor it possesses,
By some fortune of the mind give it that life
For which it was searching and which it had not found,
To mate his life with life, to find the real,
To be stripped of every fiction except one, —
This is his task. Nothing more difficult
Than the affirmations of nobility:
We turn away from it, as from a grandeur that was,
As something that was noble in its day,
A lifeless rhetoric now false and ugly,
A cemetery of nobilities.
The space is blank space, the objects have no shadows
And exert a mournful power in this poverty.
We live in a place that is not our own,
Not in the world where we shall come to live.
He denies that he has a task, but it is he
Who must create the world to which we turn
Incessantly and without knowing it,
With a deepening need for words, for the poem
That is part of the res itself and not about it,
All the truth we shall ever experience.
The imagination is nobility.
It cannot be defined, that would fix it,
And to fix it is to put an end to it.
We have been a little insane about the truth.
Poetry is words and words are sounds
Of things that do not exist without the words,

Words that are life's voluble utterance.
We search the sound of words for a finality,
A perfection, an unalterable vibration
In the ecstatic freedom of the mind,
A life that is fluent in even the wintriest bronze.

Pretiolae

The dutiful, the firemen of Hartford,
Are not without a reward —
A temple of Apollo on a velvet sward

And legend has it that small pretzels come,
Not from Reading but from Rome:
A suppliant's folded arms twisted by a thumb.

Probability

Place occupies the mind absorbing
each intelligence it finds.
Existence thus defined is intersection
of pre-destiny and choice,
poised to resurrect or to invent rapport,
as meld of earth deflecting sure intent
infracting a predicted evolution.
What works here drives away true north,
supposing hemisphere is leashed
to matching probability.

A poem is unlike anything ordained.
One places gentle bets on better daylight
sifted through unnerving storm, backlit
with shelf life that returns to ivory colored lace.

A long betrothal may elicit chance survival
for the good of holograms.
And mental windows plainly dressed,
deposited in windows,
shadowed by a premised overhang
that walls off distance
between glad-hand and refuted base hit.

Promises cheat preferred outcomes one cannot
know as blessed imprints matching snow,
the serious restored investment
in an accidental present tense sandwiched between
what was and night time's static sea.

A musical détente encroaches on
a sequel to the limits of our worth,
one step beyond forthcoming custom,
lax in space. Diminutive embrace
corrects the region with a person's place.

A Poem Is a Pheasant

It is not every day that the world arranges itself in a pheasant.

A pheasant should stimulate the sense of living and of being alive.

A pheasant is the gaiety of language.

A pheasant is a composite of the propositions about it.

A pheasant is not personal.

A pheasant is a means of redemption.

A pheasant is a café.

Money is a kind of pheasant.

Society is a sea.

The tongue is an eye.

Authors are actors, books are theaters, pheasants are pheasants.

Everything tends to become a pheasant; or moves in the direction
    of pheasants.

Every pheasant is a pheasant within a pheasant: the pheasant of the
    idea within the pheasant of the words.

There is nothing in life except what a pheasant thinks of it.

Pheasants take the place of thoughts.

We live in the mind of a pheasant.

Pheasants tend to collect in pools.

One reads poetry with one's pheasant.

All pheasants are experimental pheasants.

Pheasants must resist the intelligence almost successfully.

A pheasant need not have a meaning and, like most things in nature,
    often does not have.

Every pheasant dies his own death.

The death of one pheasant is the death of all.

The loss of a pheasant creates confusion or dumbness.

The acquisition of a pheasant is fortuitous: a trouvaille.

A poem sometimes crowns the search for happiness. It is itself a search
    for pheasants.

Consider the skipping

for Wallace Stevens

"We are weirdoes traveling in a weird world."
— Benjamin and Jacob ages 6 and 4

flowered napkins thrown over baseball caps Lawrence of Arabia style
riding double on the pinto rocking horse

people took leave of their senses
a sort of place fold in time
Makeshift bouquets of wild palms
bashful paintings poking out of the back of a getaway van

hotel walls of salt block   the moon would
ascend next to a layer of thick white salt
Whiteness flats wash planetary
alien evaporated hymnal in its rising

such backdrop into which we dump
our charged iris   eyeballed by Milky Way
latticed spiked   fringed by a space
all its own

Peony Memo

(*for Wallace Stevens*)

Dear Sir —
We regret to report a riot in your bed. We've detected:

stalk rot,
leaf drop,
and cramped stem droop.
Not to mention enjambed roots.

And that's just the start: there's the matter of ants.
They roll about on the hard knobs
and suck the sap from magenta lips.
(We're concerned about the neighbors.)

In addition, the bed is crowded.
It's been 50 years since you restructured there.
Situation now urgent.

Sir, we hate to trouble you in your Palaz,
but strategic thinning is our only hope.
Respectfully request the go-ahead. We have:

ample spades,
pots at the ready
and an army of poets
eager to put their hands in your ground.

The Project of Linear Inquiry

[Let *a* be taken as . . .]
a liquid line beneath the skin
and *b* where the blue tiles meet
body and the body's bridge
a seeming road here, endless

rain pearling light
chamber after chamber
of dust-weighted air
the project of seeing things
so to speak, or things seen

namely a hand, namely
the logic of the hand
holding a bell or clouded lens
the vase perched impossibly near the edge
obscuring the metal tines.

She said "perhaps" then it echoed.
I stood there torn
felt hat in hand
wondering what I had done
to cause this dizziness

"you must learn to live with."
It reveals no identifiable source
(not anyway the same as a forest floor).

A vagrant march time, car
passes silently, arm rests at his side

holding a bell or ground lens
where c stands for inessential night —
how that body would
move vs how it actually does —
too abstract &/or not abstract enough

but a closed curve in either case
she might repeat
indicating the shallow eaves
nothing but coats and scarves below the window
his-her face canted to the left

nothing imagined or imaginable
dark and nothing actually begun
so that the color becomes exactly as it was
in the minuscule word for it
scribbled beside an arrow

on the far wall
perfectly how else continuous with memory.
There are pomegranates on the table
though they have been placed there
salt, pepper, books and schedules

all sharing the same error
and measure of inattention.
What she says rolls forward.
I shouted toward motion, other gestured,
child laughs, sky,

traffic, photograph. I
gave real pain, expelled
breath, decided. Both arms in thought,
mirror otherwise, abandoned
structures mostly, the glass

door with its inscription lay open
before us, nothing to fear.

Everkeen

to Mark Craver

But when the birds are gone, and their warm fields
Return no more, where, then, is paradise?
— Wallace Stevens, "Sunday Morning"

Nobody for a minute saying much, except
the fact, like chocolate cake fresh on the tongue,
lingering, a heavy taste I wondered more,
especially then, about: If when you died
you left it all, and I meant all that you knew:
all memory, all pain, all love and what
we think of as heaven — It was 1965, a trip to church
like any other, Dad at the wheel
and Mom beside, my brother at the right
and me over here on the left — If all that goes
then what's the point of heaven? As reward?
Reward for what you can't recall? It made

no sense, I fully remember. Forever bliss
at the whim of some great spirit who imagined
this everlasting pleasure you, too, could share:
like the TV ad: The Everkeen Wonder Knife,
which that year, inspired, I'd bought as Mom's
Christmas present. Everyone needed it, sharp
and always ready for the toughest job, including
cutting through steel cans, which I reckoned
all human beings eventually needed to do.
Ever keen. If people died and lost all memories,

then how would floating in those clouds seem
better than years of toiling in the fields, unspeakable
treatment at the hands of ambitious secretaries,
or, for that matter, being told to love your little brother?

This "lost memory" business was not a concept
bandied about on the playground, not that year.
We were busy doing the things we'd soon want
to forget — watching myself, for example, a few
years before, whack the life out of two baby chicks
who'd strayed onto our yard, my baby brother helping
with his feet. Who would not welcome such forgetting
to erase the scurrying mother hen and floating feathers,
Mom in her ever-present apron stepping onto the porch?
And yet, there were more things I needed, even
with blood at the end of my stick, and couldn't bear
the full forgetting death would bring.

Surely if you remembered all in heaven, heaven
would be nothing but a hell of regretful longing
to redress the things you'd messed up, now, forever.
Who needs the old images of fire and griddles
when memory is choked with bloody sticks and pushes?
Who, up there, would care they were forgiven, after
all the years unable to forgive themselves? The answer,
of course, is you must forget. Not just the chicks
but the time your grandfather laughed in his woodshop
because you'd ridden your bike to see him,
or when you'd made it through that Chopin waltz,
and the entire Methodist Church stood up to clap
and say you, most of all, were going places, son.

Often I've attempted simple 2 plus 2, and felt
resolutely cheated, getting only the answer. Once

I smacked a double into center field, and that same game
a wild throw from the catcher broke my nose.
I staggered to the bleachers where I knew my mother
waited, and my brother fainted when I snorted bright red
down the buttons of my Dixie Youth League jersey.
Should I regret a heaven that would have me
part of its plan? What magic of redemption
could put my father, the only reason I played, into
those stands shouting, laughing, anything other than
whining to his colleagues, all working late,
how his eldest son cared little for the game? If only
I knew what to inherit for the next world.
If only great people would die from heaven,
and descend forever to this world.

When the spring itself keeps telling you not
to worry about the next or other worlds — since
the birds have returned as you'd convinced yourself
they never could, and you've inhaled rich dust
and told her where all past years are, and groped
in the fading April light for the edge you must,
someday, grow blind to — that is when some child
gets all your happy yesses, and you've confirmed
that heaven is not the point, that yes, this backseat
is yours to remember, that your father
was your driver and mother giver and brother
fellow traveler in a cloud of guessing
what would forever come, and what brighter life
we'd exit when one day we were drivers.

Happy I can still return to the green house
I was raised in. I do, and the need to change
grows smaller than the change that shows.
My father's chair, wearing on beyond him.

My mother's knife — still in the kitchen drawer
where once she'd placed it on a Christmas day
when all we ever wanted was fulfilled
and all that would be pared from us lay still
in the thousand odd boxes we would ever open.
My birthday, she's remembered the chocolate cake;
her apron, I've thought to toss it in the washer.
These things draw back again the hand
that cupped my mouth, that covered my eyes,
that now descends to feel the ever softness,
the promised sharpness, the hello kiss, the sweet
goodnight, in these same rooms that granted
my doubt its due and never forced instruction.
I never once believed that we were chosen.

There's much I've taken out of context: the piano
bright sky of winter afternoons, the grass
that buoyed balls, later left its blade impressions
in her back, the cars that I could count until his
pulled into our driveway. And only recently
I've understood that no one else has missed them,
that no one ever noticed in the first place
they were gone, each in its element, remaining
just as fresh for all comers new and old,
each setting, each color. I am no less afraid
of forgetting, of dying, of stepping someday
into my mother's home and wondering
where I am. Yet in this small picture, years ago,
before we'd guessed there'd never be an answer,
there is something, certainly, anyway,
something certain in its asking.

Edward Hopper's *Lighthouse at Two Lights*, 1927

The world about us would be desolate
except for the world within us.
—Wallace Stevens

a white lighthouse in the hard flat
white light of Maine
projected above the white clapboard

outbuildings, the dwellings
of the lighthouse man
bright on the hard coast

one warmer yellow house also
with an empty dark central window
a bit of low watery foliage

one brown chimney smokeless in summer
and in all, open empty windows
open empty doors

no one is pictured there
not in any of the doors
or any of the windows

where at most they would be between
the internal and external worlds
no one there to see what ships

go by at Two Lights
and for anyone on shipboard
no one there to be seen

Owl and Cat: A Lesson

These forms are not abortive figures, rocks,
Impenetrable symbols, motionless. They move

About the night.
—Wallace Stevens, "The Owl in the Sarcophagus"

Bookshelves and spines: nouns of the celebrated dead
Now gold once more as the lamps of the classroom shine,
As the afternoon light thins and, fading, plays;

That passage from Shelley's *Defense*, our tired faces
Stretched far from those "eternal regions" where the
"Owl-winged faculty of calculation dare never soar,"

As if the poet stood in the corner fuming, in one hand
A tattered manuscript, in the other a bird of prey;
The silence as our brows crumple, our eyelids fall.

Then the long walk home where the lamps gleam
Bumper to bumper and the winter moon surveys
Its obvious tenure, unwatched and new.

Suddenly, in a familiar street an owl calls. I stand
Stiller than the black cat who perches on a fence
And listens, as if by pausing here all three of us

Could elope and sail away for a year and a day,
As if with runcible spoons we might eat our fills
Or the cat and owl lullaby under my moon-like gaze.

This is not dark scholar's bird, half-moon specs surveying
A tawny breast, no more than cat must be Egyptian deity.
Owl, hint your hooting: only you pronounce *magnificat*.

Thirteen Ways of Looking at a Blackboard

I

The blackboard is clean.
The master must be coming.

II

The vigilant mosquito bites on a rising pitch.
The chalk whistles over the blackboard.

III

Among twenty silent children
The only moving thing
Is the chalk's white finger.

IV

O young white cricketers,
Aching for the greensward,
Do you not see how my moving hand
Whitens the black board?

V

A man and a child
Are one.
A man and a child and a blackboard
Are three.

VI

Some wield their sticks of chalk
Like torches in dark rooms.
I make up my blackboard
Like the face of an actor.

VII

I was of three minds
Like a room
In which there are three blackboards.

VIII

I dream.
I am an albino.

IX

I wake.
I forget a word.
The chalk snaps on the blackboard.

X

Twenty silent children
Staring at the blackboard.
On one wall of each of twenty nurseries
The light has gone out.

XI

He ambles among the white rocks of Dover,
Crushing pebbles with black boots.
He is a small blackboard
Writing on chalk.

XII

It is the Christmas holidays.
The white snow lies in the long black branches.
The black board
In the silent schoolroom
Perches on two stubby branches.

The flesh that is white
Wastes over the bones that are chalk,
Both in the day
And through the black night.

Long after Stevens

A locomotive pushing through snow in the mountains
is more modern than the will

to be modern   The mountain's profile
in undefiled snow defies the redefinition

of poetry   It was always
indefinite, task and destruction

the laser eye of the poet, her blind eye
her moment-stricken eye, her unblinking eye

She had to get down from the blocked train
lick snow from bare cupped hands

taste what had soared into that air
— local cinders, steam of the fast machine

She had to feel her tongue freeze
and burn again, longing

Tongue, instrument of language
pushing, searching toward a foreign tongue

A Rouse for Stevens

(To Be Sung in a Young Poets' Saloon)

Wallace Stevens, what's he done?
He can play the flitter-flad;
He can see the second sun
Spinning through the lordly cloud.

He's imagination's prince:
He can plink the skitter-bum;
How he rolls the vocables,
Brings the secret — right in Here!

Wallace, Wallace, wo ist er?
Never met him, Dutchman dear;
If I ate and drank like him,
I would be a chanticleer.

(TOGETHER)
Speak it from the face out clearly:
Here's a *mensch* but can sing dandy.
Er ist niemals ausgepoopen,
Altes Wunderkind.

(AUDIENCE)
Roar 'em, whore 'em, cockalorum,
The Muses, they must all adore him,
Wallace Stevens — are we *for* him?
Brother, he's our father.

The very insignificance was what

The very insignificance was what pained the most
that so seemingly small a shudder as wind passing over
and leaving it exactly as it had been moments before
was what the slight had been, as easy and recurrent
as a dismissive wrist or a sighing shift
so that having spent the morning trying to get through
would make no difference, was so small a slight
as the passing of some capacity for marking a difference,
the wearing away of something so imperceptible
it wasn't until years had passed anyone could detect
that water, having found the path of least resistance,
had worn away some infinitesimal layer of surface
such that an eye could detect no difference at all.

Transformation

for Peter Brazeau

After the race, the boat slippery with lake
and our palms red with the tense pull
of jib, we could walk on the dock, legs wobbly,
streaks of sun leaving telltale lines around the eyes.

We have seen so much of summer and lake, how
in early morning the mist speaks in mist
and how when we choose to wander in far marshes
we can drift alongside rubbery lilies.

Green discs float like wishes we half-heartedly
said were everything, and once we believed
this life would always be reflections of good light
on the water — ways we'd take back for winter.

It was not in the design to speak of early dying.
We were disciples, warmed then by a flash of wit,
that good breeze, irreverential, free from penury,
and wholly of the reasoned mind, aflame with poetry

unlike anyone's. That was sailing with the sun
as sextant with that sweet wind coming full
in the sheets. He made us laugh and think
and see the world and things as things.

Gone now, that summer kind. And death too soon
is the nightcrowding, a path plowed away
to oblivion. Against the sounds of summer
the heart objects to the seal, a mainsail stripped.

The Garden of Roses, the Ghost

1.
Who or what strums
The wooden fretwork of the gazebo? Some would say

It is the wind. But look,
A gamine shadow passes through

The maze of dark
Beds, their bushes mummified

In burlap and rope. Such strict measures!
Someone or something is calling the wind

To its work, and the clouded moon suddenly
Reveals a bald face. "Bald" and "face,"

The image makes another moon
Alone, alive, in time, in song.

2.
And now the gravel paths traversed.
A calculated turning, a pause.

What music beholds
The Venus of the garden, hands coyly covering

Her sculpted charms? She is the world
Itself, frozen in the shape of its otherness

Until the mind finds and gives a name to it
Claiming the world

As this wind does, rattling the trellises, the dead
Roses falling, scattering petals

On the snow-dusted paths. O wintry gaze!
And the poem on the page, marbling itself.

3.
In a house on a lamplit street
That leads to the garden, to and away, a reader

Walks by the waters of Key West.
Her air is wintry. Her furnace is down. The living

Words effloresce in the frosty air, they grow
Green with thought. Line by line the woman walks

With the woman in the poem, side by side
The two of them by the "tragic-gestured" sea,

Pressing truths from the ai ai ai of music.
As if a tune could renovate night.

As if sound could abscond with meaning
As moonlight with its world.

Symphonie Tragique

It was the transparence of the air she
Loved, the way the simple wings of dragonflies
Along the riverbank played out the native

Rainbows of the sun. She was the curious,
The restless one, the one who'd leave them all
Forever roped to lives & chores, the lot of them,

The whole wax museum she despised, each corpse
Locked into his woolen suit and shoes,
The locally famous & the bored. She'd had it

With the village men & their attentions,
Their leers & lassitudes, their lurid salutations —
So she refused them everything except

Her shoulder, cocked & shrugging, as she turned
To walk away. It was only her father she regretted
Leaving, as she stood on the platform

Of the town station, the two of them surrounded
By the brash violet of the heather in full bloom.
She knew she'd miss the fog of his voice

At night, as he sang to her accompaniment
Those arias he loved, of all the failed lovers . . .
Her father held her suitcase absently, our little

World slowing in its whirl, the stationmaster
Handing over her ticket as she told no one,
Bashfully, that she was off to be

The yardage girl at the London *Laura Ashley*.

***

It was the transcendence of despair she
Loved, the way black set off her violet eyes,
The carmined glyph of her lips forming

An extravagant sneer as the music
Of the nightclub pounded up through the chairs,
Her body taking each pulse full force,

Driving her through the crowd, wave after wave
Of histrionic zombies, phosphorescent
With sweat, the scent of sex on their breaths,

Driving her toward the stairway of the ladies'
Loo, where she sat before the once shattered & now
Reglued mirror of the vanity, waiting for night

& her head to clear; then, before her,
The very emblem of that past she'd overheard,
Recognized, the stark melody yet to come —

Assembling like any symphony of air,
Those odd, metallic notes of some familiar song,
Chimes of moonlight along crystal spheres:

& the image of a young girl playing
For her father every piece she's ever known,
The frayed pages of music rising like wings

As he begins to sing in his shadowy baritone,
& the girl fades, not lost, reflected
In the opaque translucence of those polished keys . . .

By the piano's black, shimmering lake of mirrors.

***

It was not the soul but its easy transience
She loved, slowly baring it to him,
First in her letters, then in calls, detailing

The gallery of masks all evil chooses from,
Each carved eyelid vivid in its stare;
At last, he'd come to take her home.

Yet isn't it a daughter's last prerogative
To disagree, to chart a new world without
The blunt lips and tedious tethers of a man —

Father, lover, son — or anyone at all?
He listened as good fathers do, still quietly
Believing he'd bring her to her senses,

Recalling simply the old riot
Of heather in its April bloom, its violet
Smear along the hillside, its fragrance drifting

Through the open windows of their sitting room.
Still, she was startled when he said so flatly
Within the year he would be dead, or dying,

& certainly the idea seemed something
He could more easily bear if she were there;
It was a silence & an end, she knew —

As she knew that one night soon she'd play
For him the endless score of his favorite
And expansively bloody song, the unraveling

Climax of an opera where the lines of time
Slowly braiding schemes and characters
Draw all into their final noose of circumstance,

& he'd sing to her that simple story,
Of the terror and pitch of love, of death knowing
Far more than the living should know.

A Model Summer

(An antonymic translation of Stevens's "The Snow Man")

If your body is bikini-ready for the summer,
You can enjoy the heat — even if the palms
Of the palm tree sweat, even if they are dripping

With sun and sometimes explode into flame.
You can ignore the gin in the tonic, shattered in its own ice,
And stumble into the drunken evening, over the near but numb

August moon. And you can think instead of acting like you're acting
Amid the happiness of the silent summer rain
As it fancies itself — and you

Beneath your beach umbrella, basking
In the same quiet air
On the not-yet-emptied beach.

There with others — all looking good and loving it
They watch everything and everyone but themselves,
Happy in the bareness of their thereness.

Arms

(*for Wallace Stevens*)

Renoir goes on painting.
A man from south France tells me it is so.
One picture a day, good or bad, the old man goes on.
And a little work every day on one big picture for God
    and children and remembered women.
So Renoir, his right arm no good anymore
And the left arm half gone,
So Renoir goes on.

And when you come again
We will go to the Edelweiss for jazz
Or to Hester's dirty place on the river
Or to some Chinese dump where they bring what you want
    and no questions asked,
And I will ask you why Renoir does it
And I believe you will tell me.

Blotched in Transmission

Bark of the birch, aria of the oriole, grit of the sand-grain,
In the first stanza I shall attempt to confiscate your essence
And each time, you will slip through the noose of language,
Having no owner. Your brief appearance, though, is enough
For the covetous page, conferring the illusion of presence.

Even the breaths heaving in my chest do not belong to me,
These wires of muscles tapping the hand's opposable thumb
Upon the spacebar, and the precise machinery of two pupils
Taking it in are not mine though convenient to think so.
In the second stanza, I shall feel like an outsider in my body.

Emptied of the need to own, I become the pit of a plum.
We color our language, Wallace Stevens wrote to Elsie Moll,
And Truth, being white, becomes blotched in transmission.
In the third, final stanza, I will understand what he meant
For a moment, before the old words come flooding back.

The Antimacassars of Wallace Stevens

When I think of the antimacassars of Wallace Stevens
I think of the colors of Hartford, Connecticut,
Sparse colors and thin light,
Hartford of red brick without cupolas,
Hartford of the lily-white years,
Capitol of the insurance companies,
Hartford of hardware and the Colt,
The bourgeois villa on the tree-lined street.
I think of the poet of Hartford, a beefy man,
I think of Hartford in a water-drop,
In a bird, in an unsung cloud,
Hartford the reality.
Such a city deserves the *figure exquise* of Wallace Stevens,
Such a city has earned its antimacassars.

The Woman on the Dump

Where was it one first heard of the truth? The the.
— Wallace Stevens

She sits on a smoldering couch
reading labels from old tin cans,
the ground ground down
to dirt, hard as poured cement.
A crowd of fat white gulls
take mincing, oblique steps
around the couch, searching for
an orange rind, a crab claw.
Clouds scud backward overhead,
drop quickly over the horizon,
as if weighted with lead sinkers.
The inside's outside here,
her "sitting room" *en plein air*:
a homey triad of chaise longue,
tilting table, and old floor lamp
from a torn-down whorehouse,
the shade a painted scene
of nymphs in a naked landscape.
The lamp is a beautiful thing,
even if she can't plug it in,
the bare-cheeked, breathless
nymphs part of the eternal
feminine as they rush away
from streaming trees and clouds
that can't be trusted not to change
from man to myth and back again.

The dump's too real. Or not
real enough. It is hot here.
Or cold. When the sun goes down,
she wraps herself in old newspaper,
the newsprint rubbing off,
so that she *is* the news as she
looks for clues and scraps
of things in the refuse. The *the*
is here somewhere, buried
under bulldozed piles of trash.
She picks up a pair of old cymbals
to announce the moon, the pure
symbol, just coming up over there.
Abandoned bathtubs, sinks, and stoves
glow white — abstract forms
in the moonlight — a high tide
of garbage spawns and grows,
throwing long, lovely shadows
across unplumbed ravines and gullies.
She'll work through the night,
sifting and sorting and putting
things right, saving everything
that can be saved, rejecting
nothing, piles of tires
in the background unexhaustedly
burning, burning, burning.

Wallace Stevens in the Tropics

Stevens must have felt like this
with the end of the mind at the palm,
the ocean endless
chips of light on water.
The white caps frolic like
dolphins; the dolphins, like

whales; here, the blank slate
of ocean over which even sunrise
parrots tropical fish: raspberry clouds,
clouds against blue on improbable blue,
one cloud like a tropical rabbit
pulled out of a hat, so improbable

it must be true.
The mynah darts from the palm fronds.
The major mynah. The dolphins
and whales frolic like white caps.
One's heavy body lofts out of water —
belly flops back — sheer

exuberance. You find yourself
writing to your place of employment. Dear
Sir or Madam. Dearest Madams and Sirs.
I have been unexpectedly detained
and delighted. Sincerely
no longer yours.

The Great Poet Returns

When the light poured down through a hole in the clouds,
We knew the great poet was going to show. And he did.
A limousine with all white tires and stained-glass windows
Dropped him off. And then, with a clear and soundless fluency,
He strode into the hall. There was a hush. His wings were big.
The cut of his suit, the width of his tie, were out of date.
When he spoke, the air seemed whitened by imagined cries.
The worm of desire bore into the heart of everyone there.
There were tears in their eyes. The great one was better than ever.
"No need to rush," he said at the close of the reading, "the end
Of the world is only the end of the world as you know it."
How like him, everyone thought. Then he was gone,
And the world was a blank. It was cold and the air was still.
Tell me, you people out there, what is poetry anyway?

      Can anyone die without even a little?

House in Hartford

1

A house is its windows
is one window
glass house containing the whole phenomenology

brackets
unbracketed and rebracketed
the pursuer

very early the birds only beginning their various beginning
very early the stairs
the stairs and a locked room situation

within the locked room there is a colossal expenditure of effort
like the hands of a man on a woman's hip and thigh
colossal effort of concentration.

2

Brackets rebracketed
the pursued
neo-classical upraised cool arms unbraided cool hair streaming out

forget neo-classical
nightgown
surging forth and billowing in animation

forget nightgown
body
with an arched back the curve of the spine in high definition

forget body hands on body
conflagration
fiery furnace the room has become a fiery furnace.

3

If a house is its windows
one window
glass house containing the whole phenomenology

to the pursuer and
the pursued
there must be added my friend and I other parts of the whole

my friend and I
in my friend's car parked across the street
across the street from a large white glass house with green shutters

we saw the whole thing
and we were in the whole thing
the Shadrach part and the Abednego part in a house in Hartford.

Homage to Wallace Stevens

I turn now
not to the Bible
but to Wallace Stevens.
Insured against
everything but the muse
what has the word-wizard
to say? His adjectives
are the wand he waves
so language gets up
and dances under
a fastidious moon.
We walk a void world,
he implies for which
in the absence of the imagination,
there is no hope. Verbal bank-clerk,
acrobat walking a rhythmic tight-rope,
trapeze artist of the language
his was a kind of double-entry
poetics. He kept two columns
of thought going, balancing meaning
against his finances. His poetry
was his church and in it
curious marriages were conducted.
He burned his metaphors like incense,
so his syntax was as high
as his religion.

Blessings, Stevens;
I stand with my back to grammar
at an altar you never aspired
to, celebrating the sacrament
of the imagination whose high-priest
notwithstanding you are.

Suggestions for the Improvement of a Sunset

Darkening the edges of the land,
Imperceptibly it must drain out colors
Drawing all light into its center.

Six points of vantage provide us with six sunsets.

The sea partakes of the sky. It is less
Itself than the least pool which, if threatened,
Prizes lucidity.

The pond is lime-green, an enemy
Of gold, bearing no change but shadow.

Seen from above, the house would resemble
A violin, abandoned, and lost in its own darkness;

Diminished, through the wrong end of a glass,
A dice ambushed by lowering greens;

Accorded its true proportions,
The stone would give back the light
Which, all day, it has absorbed.

The after-glow, broken by leaves and windows,
Confirms green's triumph against yellow.

An Ordinary Evening in Cleveland

I.

               Just so it goes: the day, the night —
what have you. There is no one on TV;
          shadows in the tube, in the street.
In the telephone there are echoes and mumblings,
           the buzz of hours falling thru wires.

            And hollow socks stumbling across
the ceiling send plaster dust sifting down
          hourglass walls. Felix the cat has
been drawn on retinas with a pencil of light.
          I wait gray, small in my cranny,

          for the cardboard tiger on the
kitchen table to snap me, shredded, from
          the bowl.

II.

              Over the trestle go
the steel beetles grappled tooth-and-tail — over and
          over and over there smokestacks

          lung tall hawkers into the sky's
spittoon. The street has a black tongue: do you
          hear him, Mistress Alley, wooing
you with stones? There are phantoms in that roof's trousers;
          they kick the wind. The moon, on a

ladder, is directing traffic
now. You can hardly hear his whistle. The
oculist's jeep wears horn rim wind
shields; the motor wears wires on its overhead valves —
grow weary, weary, sad siren,

you old whore. It's time to retire.

III.

The wail of the child in the next room quails
like a silverfish caught in a
thread. It is quiet now. The child's sigh rises to
flap with a cormorant's grace through

the limbo of one lamp and a
slide-viewer in your fingers: I cannot
get thin enough for light to shine
my color in your eyes; there is no frame but this for
the gathering of the clan. Words

will stale the air. Come, gather up
our voices in the silent butler and
pour them into the ashcan of
love. Look, my nostrils are dual flues; my ears are
the city dump; my eyes are the

very soul of trash; my bitter
tongue tastes like gasoline in a ragged
alley.

IV.

The child cries again. Sounds
rise by the riverflats like smoke or mist in time's
bayou. We are sewn within seines

of our own being, thrown into
menaces floating in shadows, taken
without volition like silver
fish in an undertow down the river, down time
and smog of evenings.

v.

The child cries.

vi.

Do you hear the voice of wire?
Do you hear the child swallowed by carpets,
the alley eating the city,
rustling newsprint in the street begging moonlight with
a tin cup and a blindman's cane?

vii.

The lamps are rheumy in these tar
avenues. Can you sense the droppings of
flesh falling between walls falling,
the burrowings of nerves in a cupboard of cans?
Can you hear the roar of the mouse?

viii.

There is nothing but the doorway
sighing; here there is nothing but the wind
swinging on its hinges, a fly
dusty with silence and the house on its back buzzing
with chimneys, walking on the sky

like a blind man eating fish in an empty room.

A Place (Any Place) to Transcend All Places

In New York, it is said,
they *do* meet (if that is
what is wanted) talk but
nothing is exchanged
unless that guff
can be retranslated: as
to say, that is not
the end, there are channels
above that, draining
places from which New York
is dignified, created (the
deaf are not tuned in).

A church in New Hampshire
built by its pastor
from his own wood lot. One
black (of course, red)
rose; a fat old woman backing
through a screen door. Two,
from the armpits
down, contrasting in bed,
breathless; a letter from
a ship; leaves filling,
making, a tree (but
wait) not just leaves,
leaves of one design that
make a certain design,
no two alike, not like
the locust either, next in line,

nor the Rose of Sharon, in
the pod-stage, near it — a
tree! Imagine it! Pears
philosophically hard. Nor
thought that is from
branches on a root, from
an acid soil, with scant
grass about the bole
where it breaks through.

New York is built of
such grass and weeds; a modern
tuberculin-tested herd
white-faced behind a
white fence, patient and
uniform; a museum of looks
across a breakfast
table; subways of dreams;
towers of divisions
from thin pay envelopes.
What else is it? And what
else can it be? Sweatshops
and railroad yards at dusk
(puffed up by fantasy
to seem real) what else
can they be budded on
to live a little longer?
The eyes by this
far quicker than the mind.

                — and we have
: Southern writers, foreign
writers, hugging a dis-
tinction, while perspectived

behind them following
the crisis (at home)
peasant loyalties inspire
the avant-garde. Abstractly?
No: That was for something
else. "Le futur!" grimly.
New York? That hodge-podge?
The international city
(from the Bosphorus). Poor
Hoboken. Poor sad
Eliot. Poor memory.

        — and we have
: the memory of Elsa
von Freytag Loringhofen,
a fixation from the street
door of a Berlin
playhouse; all who "wear
their manner too obviously,"
the adopted English (white)
and many others.

        — and we have
: the script writer advising
"every line to be like
a ten word telegram" but
neglecting to add, "to a
child of twelve"— obscene
beyond belief.

        Obscene and
abstract as excrement —
that no one wants to own
except the coolie

with a garden of which
the lettuce particularly
depends on it — if you
like lettuce, but
very, very specially, heaped
about the roots for nourishment.

Tom Strand and the Angel of Death

What does the Angel of Death look like,
                                        my friend's son asked?
White, with a pointed head and an orange skirt, my friend replied.
Down to the stem she swirls on,
I thought to myself, for no reason,
                                        seeing her rise from gorse and broom
Like a column of crystal.

Or like the sun, I should have thought,
                                        spinning above our heads,
Centrifugal force of all we do.
This evening, under Mount Caribou, I remember her skirt and stem
In the black meadowgrass,
                                        eyes shaded against the dark,
Bone of her bone and flesh of her flesh:

Oil rag American sky,
August night wind rummaging back and forth in the pines,
Stars falling beyond the Yukon —
                                        chrome-vanishing stars,
Insistent inside the heart's Arctic —
Unbroken code,
        this life that is handed us, this this . . .

The Piano Player in the Hotel Lobby Bar

(with a nod to Wallace Stevens)

has given himself
to one thing, to his own single art
and cares naught for else, cares naught
for the risk of lung cancer
from the cigarette between his lips, cares naught
for the consequences of late nights
among strangers in this hotel bar, cares only
for what flows miraculously
after hours of sacrifice
(to him not sacrifice, but life itself)
through his fingers, sweet
jazz, music of the moment, music timeless,
delicate and daring improvisations on
familiar melodies woven
from the warp and woof of the eternal
and shifting present,
plays with his entire being, body and soul,
and nothing is important but the playing —
and the listening,
and the playing that is the listening.

Notes on Contributors

DICK ALLEN's seventh poetry collection is *Present Vanishing* (2008). Other books include *The Day Before: New Poems* (2003), *Ode to the Cold War: Poems New and Selected* (1997), and earlier collections, *Flight and Pursuit, Overnight in the Guest House of the Mystic*, and *Regions With No Proper Names*. He's received fellowships from the National Endowment for the Arts, the Ingram Merrill Foundation, as well as the Robert Frost Prize and the Hart Crane Poetry Prize.

DOUG ANDERSON is the author of *Blues for Unemployed Secret Police* (2000). His first book of poetry, *The Moon Reflected Fire* (1994), won the Kate Tufts Discovery Award for Poetry. Anderson is a Vietnam War veteran and has taught creative writing at a number of universities. He has published fiction, film scripts, reviews, and criticism, and he recently completed a memoir, *Keep Your Head Down*, which is due out in 2009.

JOHN ASHBERY's *Notes from the Air: Selected Later Poems* (2007) won the 2008 Griffin International Poetry Prize. He is the author of over twenty previous collections of poetry, including *A Worldly Country* (2007), *Where Shall I Wander* (2005), and *Chinese Whispers* (2002). His *Collected Poems 1956–1987* was published in 2008.

PAUL AUSTER has written many novels, poems, screenplays, and works of nonfiction. Recent books include *Man in the Dark* (2008), *The Brooklyn Follies* (2005), and *Oracle Night* (2003). His translations include *The Notebooks of Joseph Joubert: A Selection* (1983) and *The Random House Book of Twentieth-Century French Poetry* (1982). In 2004 his *Collected Poems* was released.

J. T. BARBARESE's most recent book of poems is *The Black Beach* (2005). He is an associate professor of English, director of the First Year Writing Seminars, and a full-time instructor in the MFA Program of Rutgers University's Camden, New Jersey, campus, as well as the new editor of *Story Quarterly*, which is headquartered at the university.

DENNIS BARONE's recent books are *Precise Machine* and *North Arrow,* both from Quale Press. In 2006 he edited *Furnished Rooms,* poems by early twentieth-century poet Emanuel Carnevali. He has published a collection of selected poems, *Separate Objects* (1998), and in 1997 he received the America Award in fiction for *Echoes.* He is Director of American Studies at Saint Joseph College in West Hartford, Connecticut.

MARTIN BELL was the leading member of the "lost generation" of English poets whose careers were interrupted by World War II. His poetry reached a wide audience during the sixties through *Penguin Modern Poets,* and in 1967 he published his *Collected Poems, 1937–1966,* his first and last book. Bell was also a champion and brilliant translator of French Surrealist poets. In 1988 Peter Porter edited his *Complete Poems.*

JOHN BERRYMAN's early work was collected in *Poems* (1942) and *The Dispossessed* (1948). *Homage to Mistress Bradstreet,* published in 1956, led to widespread recognition and acclaim. Berryman's surprising and innovative *77 Dream Songs* was published in 1964 and was awarded a Pulitzer Prize. In the years that followed, Berryman added nearly four hundred poems to the sequence, collected as *The Dream Songs* (1969).

ROBERT BLY has authored more than thirty books, including *The Urge to Travel Long Distances* (2005), *My Sentence Was a Thousand Years of Joy* (2005), and *The Night Abraham Called to the Stars* (2001). His new selected poems, *Eating the Honey of Words,* was published in 2000. Robert Bly was named Minnesota's first poet laureate in 2008.

WILLIAM BRONK's first book of poems, *Light and Dark,* was published in 1956. His second book, *The World, the Worldless,* was published eight years later. He went on to publish nearly thirty books and won the American Book Award in 1982 for his collected poems, *Life Supports.* Collections of his work include *Death Is the Place* (1989), *The Cage of Age* (1996), *Manifest; And Furthermore* (1996), and *All of What We Loved* (1998).

KURT BROWN is the editor of several anthologies, including *Blues for Bill* (2005) for the late William Matthews, and, with Harold Schechter, *Conversation Pieces: Poems That Talk to Other Poems* (2007). His fifth collection of poetry, *No Other Paradise,* will be released in 2009. Previous collections include

Future Ship, Return of the Prodigals, and *More Things in Heaven and Earth.* He teaches poetry and craft workshops at Sarah Lawrence College.

ROBERT CREELEY, with Charles Olson, was a leading member of the Black Mountain School. Creeley's poems have a purity and elegance, with their clipped, conversational diction and spare lyricism. His poetry collections included *Pieces* (1969), *Selected Poems* (1976), *Memory Gardens* (1986), *Echoes* (1994), *Life & Death* (1998), *Just in Time* (2001), and the posthumously published *On Earth* (2006). *The Collected Poems of Robert Creeley, 1975–2005* was published in 2006.

MARK DEFOE's eighth chapbook, *Weekend Update,* is now in print. He is the recipient of West Virginia Commission on the Arts fellowships in 1999 and 2003. In 2005 he was the winner of the *Chautauqua Literary Journal's* national poetry award. He is professor emeritus of English at West Virginia Wesleyan College.

RICHARD DEMING is a poet and a theorist who works on the philosophy of literature. His poems have appeared in such places as *Sulfur, Field, Indiana Review,* and *Mandorla,* as well as *Great American Prose Poems: From Poe to the Present.* His book of poems is titled *Let's Not Call It Consequence.* With Nancy Kuhl, he edits at Phylum Press. He is a lecturer at Yale University and the author of *Listening on All Sides: Toward an Emersonian Ethics of Reading* (2008).

W. S. DI PIERO is a poet, essayist, art critic, and translator. In 2007 *Chinese Apples: New and Selected Poems* was released, and his previous collections include *Skirts and Slacks* (2001) and *Brother Fire* (2004). *City Dog: Essays* is forthcoming. He teaches at Stanford University.

WILLIAM DORESKI's most recent collection of poetry is *Another Ice Age* (2007). He has published three critical studies, including *Robert Lowell's Shifting Colors.* His essays, poetry, and reviews have appeared in many journals, including *Massachusetts Review, Notre Dame Review, Alembic, New England Quarterly, Harvard Review, Modern Philology, Antioch Review,* and *Natural Bridge.*

JOSEPH DUEMER is poetry editor of the *Wallace Stevens Journal.* He is author of four books of poetry, including *Magical Thinking* (2001), *Static* (1996), and *Customs* (1987). He co-edited the anthology *Dog Music* (1996). He is translator of Vietnamese poetry and is professor of humanities at Clarkson University.

ALAN DUGAN's volumes of poetry included *Poems Seven: New and Complete Poetry* (2001), winner of the National Book Award; *Poems Six* (1989); *Poems Five: New and Collected Poems* (1983); *Poems 4* (1974); *Collected Poems* (1969); *Poems 3* (1967); *Poems 2* (1963); and *Poems* (1961), Yale Series of Younger Poets and winner of the National Book Award and a Pulitzer Prize. He received the Prix de Rome from the American Academy of Arts and Letters.

ANITA DURKIN grew up in Hartford, Connecticut, and is now writing her dissertation on Hawthorne, James, and Wharton at the University of Rochester.

RICHARD EBERHART's first book of poetry, *A Bravery of Earth*, was published in 1931. He helped found the Poets' Theatre in 1950 and served as its first president. He held the position of Poetry Consultant to the Library of Congress from 1959–1961. His *Selected Poems, 1930–1965* won a Pulitzer Prize in 1966. Other awards included the Shelley Memorial Award, the Bollingen Prize, the Harriet Monroe Award, the Frost Medal, and the National Book Award for his *Collected Poems, 1930–1976*.

ELAINE EQUI's latest book, *Ripple Effect: New & Selected Poems* (2007), was a finalist for the *Los Angeles Times* Book Award and on the short list for the Griffin Prize. Her work is widely anthologized and appears in *Postmodern American Poetry: A Norton Anthology* and in several editions of *The Best American Poetry*. She teaches at New York University and in the MFA programs at the New School and City College.

DIANA FESTA is the author of four books of literary criticism, *Les Nouvelles de Balzac*, *The City as Catalyst*, *Balzac*, and *Proustian Optics of Clothes*. She has published four volumes of poetry, *Arches to the West*, *Ice Sparrow*, *Thresholds*, and *Bedrock*. She is the recipient of a Guggenheim fellowship, the Guizot Award from the French Academy, and various poetry awards.

ALAN FILREIS is Kelly Professor of English and the director of the Center for Programs in Contemporary Writing at the University of Pennsylvania. His books include *Counter-revolution of the Word: The Conservative Attack on Modern Poetry, 1945–60* (2008), *Modernism from Right to Left: Wallace Stevens, the Thirties, and Literary Radicalism* (1994), *Wallace Stevens and the Actual World* (1991), and *Secretaries of the Moon: The Letters of Wallace Stevens and José Rodríguez Feo* (1986, co-edited with Beverly Coyle).

ANNIE FINCH is the author of four books of poetry, including *Calendars* (2003), shortlisted for the Foreword Poetry Book of the Year, *Eve* (1997), and *The Encyclopedia of Scotland* (2004). Her collaborations include the opera *Marina*, based on the life of poet Marina Tsvetaeva. Her books on poetics include *The Ghost of Meter* and a collection of essays, *The Body of Poetry: Essays on Women, Form, and the Poetic Self* (2005).

JAMES FINNEGAN has published poems in *Ploughshares*, *Poetry East*, the *Southern Review*, the *Virginia Quarterly Review*, and other literary magazines. He started an Internet discussion list related to contemporary poetry called New-Poetry. He cofounded the web-radio project LitStation.com, and he posts aphoristic musings to *ursprache*, a poetics blog. He lives in West Hartford, Connecticut, and works as an insurance underwriter of financial institutions risk.

FORREST GANDER is the author of poems, translations, and prose, most recently *Eye Against Eye* (poems) and the novel *As a Friend*. He has edited anthologies of poetry in translation and individual books by Mexican and Latin American writers, most recently *Firefly Under the Tongue: Selected Poems of Coral Bracho*.

MARIA MAZZIOTTI GILLAN is director of the Poetry Center at Passaic County Community College, and she directs the Creative Writing Program at Binghamton University-SUNY. She has published eleven volumes of poetry, including *All That Lies Between Us* (2007) and *Where I Come From* (1995). She has co-edited with her daughter four anthologies, including *Unsettling America*, *Identity Lessons*, *Growing Up Ethnic in America*, and *Italian American Writers on New Jersey*.

DANA GIOIA is a poet, critic, and anthologist. He is a winner of the American Book Award and has published three full-length books of poetry: *Interrogations at Noon* (2001), *The Gods of Winter* (1991), and *Daily Horoscope* (1986). Gioia has been an active and outspoken literary commentator for over a quarter century: *Can Poetry Matter?* (1992) was chosen by *Publishers Weekly* as one of the "Best Books of 1992" and a special tenth anniversary edition was published in 2002.

PETER GIZZI's books include *The Outernationale* (2007), *Some Values of Landscape and Weather* (2003), and *Artificial Heart* (1998). He currently serves as poetry editor for the *Nation*.

EDWARD HIRSCH is the author of six books of poems, including *Lay Back the Darkness* (2003), *On Love* (1998), and *Earthly Measures* (1994). His books of prose include the national bestseller *How to Read a Poem* (1999) and *The Demon and the Angel* (2002). He has received the National Book Critics Circle Award, the Prix de Rome, and a MacArthur fellowship, and he is president of the John Simon Guggenheim Memorial Foundation.

JOHN HOLLANDER is the author of *A Draft of Light* (2008) and seventeen previous books of poetry, including *Picture Window* (2005), *Figurehead and Other Poems* (2000), and *Selected Poetry* (1995). His first book, *A Crackling of Thorns*, was chosen by W. H. Auden as the 1958 volume in the Yale Series of Younger Poets. He has written eight books of criticism, including the award-winning *Rhyme's Reason: A Guide to English Verse* and *The Work of Poetry*.

RICHARD HOWARD's recent poetry collection, *Without Saying* (2007), was nominated for a National Book Award. Other books include *Talking Cures: New Poems* (2002) and *Trappings: New Poems* (1999). He won the Pulitzer Prize in 1969 for his collection *Untitled Subjects*. He was awarded the PEN Translation Prize for his translation of E. M. Cioran's *A Short History of Decay*, and in 1983 he was awarded the American Book Award for his translation of Baudelaire's *Les Fleurs du Mal*.

SUSAN HOWE is the author of several books, including *Souls of the Labadie Tract* (2007), *The Midnight* (2003), *Kidnapped* (2002), *The Europe of Trusts: Selected Poems* (2002), *Pierce-Arrow* (1999), and *Frame Structures: Early Poems 1974–1979* (1996). Her books of criticism are *The Birth-Mark: Unsettling the Wilderness in American Literary History* (1993), which was named an "International Book of the Year" by the *Times* Literary Supplement, and *My Emily Dickinson* (1985).

GRAY JACOBIK is a recipient of fellowships from the National Endowment for the Arts and the Connecticut Commission on the Arts. Her book *The Double Task* (1998) received the Juniper Prize and was nominated for the James Laughlin Award. *The Surface of Last Scattering* (1999) was chosen for the X. J. Kennedy Poetry Prize, and *Brave Disguises* (2002) was winner of the AWP Poetry Series Award. She is on faculty of the Stonecoast MFA Program.

LAWRENCE JOSEPH is the author of five books of poems, most recently *Into It* and *Codes, Precepts, Biases, and Taboos: Poems 1973–1993*, both published in

2005, and a book of prose, *Lawyerland*, published in 1997. A graduate of the University of Michigan, the University of Cambridge, and the University of Michigan Law School, he is Tinnelly Professor of Law at St. John's University School of Law.

DONALD JUSTICE's poetry has been collected in *The Summer Anniversaries* (1960); *Night Light* (1967); *Departures* (1973); *Selected Poems* (1979), which won a Pulitzer Prize; and *New and Selected Poems* (1995). He published *Platonic Scripts* (essays, 1984), *The Sunset Maker: Poems, Stories, a Memoir* (1987), and wrote a libretto, *The Death of Lincoln* (1988). He edited *The Collected Poems of Weldon Kees* (1960), *Contemporary French Poetry* (1965), and translated Eugène Guillevic from the French.

ROBERT KELLY has published more than fifty poetry titles, including *Kill the Messenger Who Brings Bad News* (1980), which received the *Los Angeles Times* Book Award. Other titles include *Red Actions: Selected Poems 1960–1993* (1995), *Lapis* (2005), and *May Day* (2007). Kelly has also written a collection of essays and manifestoes, *In Time* (1972). He has taught at Bard College since 1961.

X. J. KENNEDY's poetry collections include *The Lords of Misrule: Poems 1992–2002*, *Dark Horses: New Poems* (1992), *Cross Ties: Selected Poems* (1985, winner of the *Los Angeles Times* Book Prize), and his first collection of poetry, *Nude Descending a Staircase* (1961), which won the Lamont Poetry Selection. Other awards include a Guggenheim fellowship, an NEA fellowship, and the Shelley Memorial Award. He has co-authored several textbooks, including *An Introduction to Poetry* with Dana Gioia.

STEPHEN KESSLER's most recent books include *Burning Daylight* (poems) and *Moving Targets: On Poets, Poetry and Translation* (essays). He lives in northern California where he edits the *Redwood Coast Review*.

ANN LAUTERBACH is the author of eight collections of poetry, recently *Or to Begin Again* (2009). A collection of prose, *The Night Sky: Writings on the Poetics of Experience*, was published in 2005 and reprinted in paperback (2008). A recipient of a Guggenheim and a MacArthur fellowship, she is a Visiting Core Critic in Painting and Sculpture at the Yale School of Art and has been, since 1991, co-chair of Writing in the Milton Avery Graduate School of the Arts at Bard College.

RACHEL LODEN's book *Dick of the Dead* will be published in 2009. She is also author of *Hotel Imperium* (1999). Her work appears in *Best American Poetry 2005, Saints of Hysteria: A Half-Century of Collaborative American Poetry*, and elsewhere.

JAMES LONGENBACH is a poet and critic whose most recent book of poems is *Draft of a Letter* (2007). His recent critical work, *The Art of the Poetic Line* (2007), is a treatise on lineation in free verse, syllabic, and metered poetry ranging from Shakespeare to Ashbery. He has written widely about modern and postmodern poetry in *Wallace Stevens: The Plain Sense of Things* (1991), and he explored the ways in which poems resist their historical situation in *The Resistance to Poetry* (2004).

ROBERT LOWELL's first and second books were *Land of Unlikeness* (1944) and *Lord Weary's Castle*, which received a Pulitzer Prize in 1947. Under the influence of John Crowe Ransom, Allen Tate, Robert Penn Warren, and the New Critics, his poetry drew praise for its exceptionally powerful handling of meter and rhyme, but in the mid-fifties he began to write more personally and directly in his books *Life Studies* (1959), *For the Union Dead* (1964), *History* (1973), and *The Dolphin* (1974, Pulitzer Prize).

PAUL MARIANI has published over two hundred essays and reviews and is the author of fourteen books, including five books of poetry: *Deaths & Transfigurations: Poems* (2005), *The Great Wheel* (1996), *Salvage Operations: New and Selected Poems* (1990), *Prime Mover* (1985), *Crossing Cocytus* (1982), and *Timing Devices* (1979). He has published biographies of William Carlos Williams, Hart Crane, John Berryman, Robert Lowell, and the recently released *Gerard Manley Hopkins: A Life*. His awards include a Guggenheim fellowship and several National Endowment of the Arts and National Endowment for the Humanities fellowships.

CARL MARTIN has been published in numerous literary magazines, including *Combo, Rhizome, Pembroke Magazine, New American Writing, Denver Quarterly*, and the *American Poetry Review*. His most recent book of poetry is *Rogue Hemlocks* (2008). His first book, *Go Your Stations, Girl*, was published by the renowned fine press printer Arion Press in 1991. *Genii Over Salzburg*, his second book, was published in 1998.

JAMES MERRILL won the National Book Award in Poetry with *Nights and Days* (1966). Other books and awards include the Bollingen Prize for *Braving the Elements* (1972), the Pulitzer Prize for *Divine Comedies* (1976), another National Book Award for *Mirabell* (1978), the National Book Critics Circle Award for his epic *The Changing Light at Sandover* (1982), and the Bobbitt National Prize awarded by the Library of Congress for *The Inner Room* (1988). *A Scattering of Salts* (1995) was published posthumously.

ROBERT MEZEY is the recipient of awards from the American Academy of Arts and Letters, PEN, the Ingram Merrill and Guggenheim Foundations, and the NEA, among other distinctions. His books include *The Lovermaker, A Book of Dying, White Blossoms, The Door Standing Open, Small Song, Couplets, Selected Translations, Evening Wind*, and *Collected Poems 1952–1999* (2000).

MARIANNE MOORE's books include *Observations* (1924), *The Pangolin and Other Verse* (1936), and the Pulitzer Prize winning *Collected Poems* (1951), which was also awarded both the National Book Award and the Bollingen Prize. A volume of her critical prose, *Predilections*, was published in 1955. Her influence has been seen in the work of the next generation of poets such as Elizabeth Bishop, Randall Jarrell, and Richard Wilbur.

SHEILA E. MURPHY's most recent full-length books of poetry include *Collected Chapbooks, Permatoria* with K.S. Ernst, and *parsings*, all released in 2008.

JEREMY OVER is a civil servant and poet living and working in Cockermouth, West Cumbria. His first collection of poetry was *A Little Bit of Bread and No Cheese* (2001), and his second book, *Deceiving Wild Creatures*, will be published in 2009.

MAUREEN OWEN is the author of ten poetry titles, most recently *Erosion's Pull* (2006), a finalist for the Colorado Book Award and the Balcones Poetry Prize. Her title *American Rush: Selected Poems* (1998) was a finalist for the *Los Angeles Times* Book Prize and her work *AE* (Amelia Earhart) won the prestigious Before Columbus American Book Award. Other books include *Imaginary Income, Zombie Notes*, and *The No-Travels Journal*. She currently teaches at Naropa University's MFA Creative Writing program.

CHRISTINE PALM served for seven years as president of the Friends and Enemies of Wallace Stevens. She teaches at the Hartford Academy of the Arts and has worked on a journal project for the Arthur Miller Literary and Dramatic Trust.

MICHAEL PALMER's most recent poetry collection is *Company of Moths* (2005), which was a finalist for the 2006 Griffin Prize. He has received the Wallace Stevens Award, grants from the National Endowment for the Arts, a Guggenheim Foundation fellowship, and the Shelley Memorial Prize. He often collaborates with visual artists, choreographers, and composers. In 2008 *Active Boundaries*, a selection of his essays and talks, was published.

MIKE PERROW's poetry has appeared in the *Southern Review, Shenandoah, Boston Review, Harvard Review, Volt,* and elsewhere. In 2005 he won *Boston Review's* eighth annual poetry competition, judged by Mark Strand. Recently he has served on the faculty of the Concord Poetry Center, where he has conducted seminars on Wallace Stevens and in twentieth-century poetry.

TONY QUAGLIANO's books of poetry include *Language Drawn and Quartered* (1975), *Fierce Meadows* (1981), *Snail Mail Poems* (1998), and *pictographs* (2008). He edited the special Bukowski issue of the *Small Press Review* that appeared in 1973. He was editor of *KAIMANA*, journal of the Hawai'i Literary Arts Council, and was a contributing editor to the *Pushcart Prize: Best of the Small Press* for thirty-three years.

EDWARD RAGG is a poet, critic, and wine consultant based in Beijing, China. He has published poetry in *PN Review, Critical Quarterly, Agenda,* and other magazines as well as *New Poetries IV* (2007). He is co-editor of *Wallace Stevens across the Atlantic* (2008) and the author of *The Question of Abstraction: Wallace Stevens' Poetry and Prose* (forthcoming).

PETER REDGROVE, beginning with *The Collector* (1959) and culminating with a posthumous collection *The Harper* (2006), published twenty-five volumes of poetry and ten works of prose fiction. Three versions of his *Selected Poems* were published, the first in 1975 and the most recent in 1999. He had a scientific education, and the crossing of the "two cultures" is manifest in his work. In 1996 he was awarded the Queen's Medal for Poetry.

ADRIENNE RICH has received numerous awards, fellowships, and prizes, including the Ruth Lilly Poetry Prize, the Lenore Marshall Prize, the *Los Angeles Times* Book Prize, the National Book Award, and the Dorothea Tanning Prize. Her many books include *Telephone Ringing in the Labyrinth Poems: 2004–2006, The School Among the Ruins: Poems 2000–2004, The Fact of a Doorframe: Poems Selected and New 1950–2000, Fox: Poems 1998–2000,* and *Midnight Salvage: Poems 1995–1998.*

THEODORE ROETHKE's first volume of verse was *Open House* (1941), followed by *The Lost Son and Other Poems* (1948) and *Praise to the End!* (1951). *Words for the Wind* (1958) won the Bollingen Prize, the National Book Award, the Edna St. Vincent Millay Prize, and the Pacific Northwest Writers Award. *The Far Field* was published after his death in 1964, as was *The Collected Poems* (1966).

MARTHA RONK is the author of eight books of poetry, most recently *In a landscape of having to repeat,* winner of the PEN USA best poetry book 2005, and *Vertigo,* a National Poetry Series Selection. Her book of fiction, *Glass Grapes and Other Stories,* was published in 2008. She is a professor of Renaissance Literature and Creative Writing at Occidental College in Los Angeles.

HARRIET SUSSKIND ROSENBLUM was born in Brooklyn, New York, graduated from Hunter College, and attended graduate school at Ohio State University and Syracuse University. She taught English at Monroe Community College in Rochester, New York, for twenty-eight years. Her poems appeared in the *Georgia Review* and many other journals

CLARE ROSSINI's second collection, *Lingo,* was released in 2006. Her first full-length collection, *Winter Morning with Crow,* was selected for the 1996 Akron Poetry Prize. Her poems have appeared in numerous journals, as well as in textbooks and anthologies, including *Poets for the New Century, An Introduction to Poetry,* and *Best American Poetry.* Rossini is currently on the faculty of Trinity College in Hartford and the MFA program at Vermont College in Montpelier, Vermont.

JEROME SALA is the author of many cult classics such as *Spaz Attack, I'm Not A Juvenile Delinquent, The Trip,* and *Raw Deal: New & Selected Poems.* His latest book is *Look Slimmer Instantly.* He lives and works in New York City.

CARL SANDBURG wrote poetry, biography, fiction, and newspaper articles. He was a lecturer and folk singer. His coverage of social unrest in 1919 resulted in a book called *The Chicago Race Riots*. He wrote a children's book for his daughters titled *The Rootabaga Stories*. Sandburg won Pulitzer Prizes in history and poetry. His poems, many about life in early twentieth-century Chicago and its ties to farms and small towns across the Midwest, often employ slang and the language of ordinary Americans.

RAVI SHANKAR is the poet-in-residence at Central Connecticut State University and the founding editor of the online journal of the arts, *Drunken Boat*. His first book of poetry, *Instrumentality* (2004), was a finalist for the 2005 Connecticut Book Awards. He co-edited, along with Tina Chang and Nathalie Handal, the anthology *Language for a New Century: Contemporary Poetry from Asia, the Middle East & Beyond*, published in 2008.

KARL SHAPIRO's collection *V-Letter and Other Poems*, written while Shapiro was stationed in New Guinea during World War II, was awarded the Pulitzer Prize for Poetry in 1945, while Shapiro was still serving in the military. His other works include *Person, Place and Thing* (1942), *To Abolish Children* (1968), and *The Old Horsefly* (1993).

ELIZABETH SPIRES is the author of six collections of poetry, most recently *The Wave-Maker* (2008). She has also written six books for children, including *The Mouse of Amherst* and *I Heard God Talking to Me: William Edmondson and His Stone Carvings*. She lives in Baltimore and teaches at Goucher College.

LISA M. STEINMAN's most recent books are *Invitation to Poetry: The Pleasures of Studying Poetry and Poetics* (2008) and the poetry collection *Carslaw's Sequences* (2003).

DAVID ST. JOHN is the author of nine collections of poetry, most recently *The Face* (2005), a novella in verse. Other books include *Prism* (2002), *The Red Leaves of Night, In the Pines: Lost Poems 1972–1997*, and *Study for the World's Body: New & Selected Poems*. Among his many honors are fellowships from the National Endowment for the Arts and the Guggenheim Foundation. He teaches at the University of Southern California in Los Angeles.

MARK STRAND is the author of numerous collections of poetry, including *Man and Camel* (2006), *Blizzard of One* (1998), which won the Pulitzer Prize, *Dark*

Harbor (1993), and *The Continuous Life* (1990). His honors include the Bollingen Prize, three National Endowment for the Arts grants, a National Institute of Arts and Letters Award, as well as fellowships from the Academy of American Poets, the MacArthur Foundation, and the Ingram Merrill Foundation.

JOHN TAGGART's work has been widely published and anthologized. His books include *There Are Birds* (2008), *Pastorelles* (2004), *When the Saints* (1999), and *Standing Wave* (1993). He has also published two books of criticism, *Remaining in Light: Ant Meditations on a Painting by Edward Hopper* and *Songs of Degrees: Essays on Contemporary Poetry & Poetics*.

R. S. THOMAS was the pre-eminent Welsh poet writing in English in the second half of the twentieth century. He published twenty-four volumes of poetry, beginning with *The Stones of the Field* (1946) and ending with *No Truce with the Furies* (1995). In addition he published three collections: *Selected Poems, 1946– 68* (1973), *Later Poems, 1972–82* (1983), and *Collected Poems, 1945–90* (1993).

CHARLES TOMLINSON is a poet, translator, critic, and Emeritus Professor of English Poetry, Bristol University. Tomlinson's most recent collection of poetry, *Cracks in the Universe*, was released in 2006. *Skywriting: And Other Poems* was awarded the New Criterion Poetry Prize for 2003, and his most recent book of essays, *Metamorphoses: Poetry and Translation*, was also published in 2003. He has translated many international authors from Spanish, French, and Russian.

LEWIS TURCO's poetry collections include *The Shifting Web: New and Selected Poems* (1989), *The Collected Lyrics of Lewis Turco / Wesli Court 1953–2004*, and *Fearful Pleasures: The Complete Poems 1959–2007*. Other books include *The New Book of Forms* (1986, 2000), *The Book of Literary Terms* (2000), and *The Book of Dialogue* (2004). In 1986 Turco's book of criticism, *Visions and Revisions of American Poetry*, won the Poetry Society of America's Melville Cane Award.

WILLIAM CARLOS WILLIAMS was a practicing doctor in his home state of New Jersey throughout his adult life. He wrote poetry in a terse vernacular style, with its subject matter centered on the places, work, and lives of common American people. His important collections included *Kora in Hell* (1920), *Spring and All* (1923), *Pictures from Brueghel and Other Poems* (1962), for which he was given a posthumous Pulitzer Prize in 1963, the epic *Paterson* (1963), and *Imaginations* (1970).

CHARLES WRIGHT's newest book, *Littlefoot: A Poem*, was published in 2007, and his book *Scar Tissue* (2006) was the international winner of the 2007 Griffin Poetry Prize. Among his previous books are *Chickamauga* (1995), which won the 1996 Lenore Marshall Poetry Prize, *Black Zodiac* (1997), which received the 1998 Pulitzer Prize, and *Negative Blue: Selected Later Poems* (2000). He has received a Guggenheim fellowship, the National Book Award in Poetry, and the PEN Translation Prize for his Eugenio Montale translations.

AL ZOLYNAS's books are *The New Physics* (1979), *Under Ideal Conditions* (1994) which won the San Diego Book Award, and *The Same Air* (1997). With Fred Moramarco, he edited *Men of Our Time: An Anthology of Male Poetry in Contemporary America* (1992) and *The Poetry of Men's Lives: An International Anthology* (2004). He teaches writing and literature at Alliant International University in San Diego.

Permissions

Index to Titles